DESIGNATED Daughter

DESIGNATED *Daughter*

· THE BONUS YEARS WITH MOM ·

D. G. Fulford with Phyllis Greene

VOICE

HYPERION
NEW YORK

Library of Congress Cataloging-in-Publication Data

Fulford, D. G.
Designated daughter : the bonus years with mom / D. G. Fulford,
with Phyllis Greene.
p. cm.
ISBN 978-1-4013-2239-7 (hardcover)
1. Fulford, D. G.   2. Greene, Phyllis.   3. Mothers and
daughters—Case studies.   4. Older women—Home care—United
States.   I. Greene, Phyllis.   II. Title.
HQ755.86.F85 2008
306.874'308460973—dc22
[B]   2007035981

Hyperion books are available for special promotions, premiums, or
corporate training. For details contact Michael Rentas, Proprietary
Markets, Hyperion, 77 West 66th Street, 12th floor, New York, New
York 10023, or call 212-456-0133.

Design by Chris Welch

First Edition

1   3   5   7   9   10   8   6   4   2

FOR BOB, FOR TIM, FOR MAGGIE

Contents

Bambi's mother had barely started to eat when abruptly she stopped and lifted her head to sniff the air. She glanced from side to side as if she were trying to hear something.

"Bambi," she whispered. But he was so busy eating that he didn't hear her.

"Bambi!" she said in terror.

Startled, Bambi looked up at her.

"The thicket!" she cried, and the two of them sprang toward the forest.

—Walt Disney's *Bambi*

DESIGNATED Daughter

DESIGNATED DAUGHTER

WHEN MY MOTHER became a widow, I became a Designated Daughter—the sibling who would try to take up the empty space that had always been filled by Dad. What I found in walking beside her was my own strong space. *Designated Daughter* is the story of what happens when a mother needs her daughter's help and the daughter gets more help in return than she could ever give.

This is my mother's story, too. She adds her voice at the end of each chapter. I'm glad you'll get to hear the insight and wisdom that has been guiding me all these years.

Designated Daughters are all over the country, all over the world. We are a secret society of women, instantly recognizable to one another. We sit in doctors' waiting rooms holding our mothers' hands. We hold the coats, we hold the purses, we hold our mothers' arms like suitors. We become so close, so bonded, we form a two-person silhouette.

My mother needed me, so I moved home to Ohio after twenty years away. Our lives began to merge and mesh. We had our glory days and our travels. I became a grandmother. She became a great-grandmother. We went to lectures, we went to lunch, we went to funerals, a lot. We have had a wondrous eight years together. Each year brings its own kind of change for my mother, and for me.

For the first five years after I came home, Mom was energetic and independent, running around like the active woman she'd been for eighty years. Then, three years ago, it was if we'd walked through a transparent door from health to sickness. She became frail, she fell in her living room, she fell in the Nordstrom parking lot. She hasn't driven for a while and can hardly walk.

But boy, can she write.

Eight years ago, my uncle Al, Mom's brother, called me in Nevada to congratulate me on my good decision to move back home. It never felt like a decision. It was the only thing my soul would let me do. I was being offered the chance to spend invaluable time with my vibrant mother, a gift of incalculable worth. Bonus years.

At my mother's knee, at middle age, I learned to celebrate knowing what you have when you have it. Each day we have together is one of poignant exaltation—the last dip in the pool at the end of a late-summer day.

You learn to read between the lines in obituaries. "Suddenly" can mean a suicide or an accident or a murder. "Unexpectedly" tweaks the imagination. "After a long illness" sends the reader rushing to the bottom of the obit, where "In lieu of flowers" reveals what the long illness was. "After a long, courageous battle" depletes me when I read it. My life has not been combative. I do not want my death to be.

Today, for the very first time, I saw my demographic referred to in an obituary. It was not defined in so many words, but a Designated Daughter can recognize another Designated Daughter anywhere.

Mrs. Lennox, eighty-seven, died. "She is survived by four children, Edward, Mark, Kenneth, and Linda, who for more than the last three years provided constant and loving care to her mother," the obituary read. There it was in print, akin to an M.D. or a Ph.D. after Linda's name. Linda had earned her D.D.

"Aren't you . . . ?" a woman asked, trying to remember my name as she wheeled her mother out of Dr. Shell's waiting room.

"Yes, I am," I said to the woman, whom I recognized from my fourth-grade class. I hadn't seen her in decades. I was guiding my own aging mother out from the elevator and in through the door.

There are daughters who, like me, work at home and have time to share, and those who are superhuman, caring and doing for a parent along with careers, commutes, children, and spouses. We are in every circumstance and walk of life. We are the people in the family who can.

Designated Daughters do the driving. We have our mother's garage-door opener on the car visor next to our own. Our mother's house key is on our key ring. We let our mother sit while we take her insurance and credit cards up to the counter for copays. We sign her name in our handwriting. We check out her library books.

Two purses on a shoulder: the universal symbol of the Designated Daughter. We walk at a slower pace, beside our mothers, or behind them when they use a wheelchair. We compliment other mothers on their fanciful canes—compliments heretofore reserved for good-looking handbags or silk scarves. We notice aluminum walkers with wheels and a seat, then we go check them out at Wal-Mart. Mom sits on the bench in front while I go off to look. A few years ago, she could jump into her car and do errands with energy left over. Now I drive on the few days she feels like going out. Sometimes she stays in the car in the parking lot. Sometimes these days break my heart.

WE HAVE OUR own cadence and language, my mother and I. We're comfortable and companionable even if we're sitting in silence. I call her at nine-thirty every morning. We have coffee together this way. We talk about war and what's for dinner.

"I'd like to report," my mother said at the end of a soul-sapping gray day in winter, "that this has been the most boring day in the history of the world."

"My mouth won't even move, it is so bored with me," I told her.

Yet we talk. We always have someone to talk to. We always have someone to listen. This is the promise we've made to ourselves—two women alone together.

One day we were having lunch at Nordstrom and saw a Designated Daughter we knew, by herself at a table. Her mother had died a few months before. The chair beside her was filled with shopping bags, but more visible, if possible, was the absence of her mother. We grabbed the daughter's hands and squeezed them on our way out. She had tears in her eyes, as did we.

—❧—

I AM THE needful mother of this Designated Daughter, and we are companions on a beautiful road to journey's end. We are not alone; lumbering along is an elephant, the pachyderm touched by the six blind men who want to know what an elephant is. Because each one touches a different part of the animal, they disagree when they attempt to describe him. Like those men, my daughter and I have different perspectives. She is fifty-seven and I am eighty-seven. Even though we walk together, the length of the road looks different to each of us, as do the hills and valleys ahead.

She is D.G., and I am Phyllis.

This elephant has a name as well.

His name is DEATH.

I hate him.

—❧—

IN MY MIND, the picture of this walk is ludicrous and makes me laugh. (In the first place, I haven't been able to walk much at all for a few years.) We both plan to ignore the elephant, but has anyone ever been able to do that? Once Debby has found a place for me to sit down, she shoos the elephant away, and we concentrate on the matters of the day. I can still (thank God) see and hear and think and speak. The white hair and the wrinkles and the shrinkage are real, but we both pretend it is a disguise.

I remember almost all of the last century and am seven years into this one. I remember that on the day we were to leave the hospital with our new baby girl, the ob/gyn left a bill on my pillow for two hundred dollars. We paid it by borrowing from her two-year-old brother's savings account! I don't have to remember the greatest generation. I *am* the greatest generation. Nostalgia is my daily reverie and the context of the bittersweet stroll we are taking.

We read so much, and think so much, and contribute so much to diseases featured in the newspapers and on TV, that describing aging, my own aging—plain old ordinary aging—is a strange exercise. It is not that easy to do, but I think it has its upside. As we write this book, there can be no sugarcoating the poignant subject matter. Once it's acknowledged, we can move beyond it, secure that it will not defeat us.

The tough part of the equation is that the days when I feel I will go on for years might be the same days D.G. has her fingers poised to call 911. As we leave a doctor's office or get a test result or I have an "episode," we each bring our own disposition, our own angle of vision, and our own frame of reference to any spot of trouble.

Knowing that, these last eight years have been a blessing in their way, not only for me but also for her. I also know the ending will be extremely traumatic. I do not worry so much about myself and what lies over the next hill that I cannot climb, literally or figuratively. I worry about Debby, this wonderful Designated Daughter who has made me the centerpiece of her life.

And that is why I hate the elephant.

2

THE CALL

I WAS LIVING IN a ghost town in the mountains of Nevada when my mother called and said I should come home. Had I known my mother then like I know her now, eight magic years later, I would have known she was calling out to me before the phone rang.

This was in early fall, September 1998. The Monica Lewinsky story was just heating up. The man I was with—the man with whom I later and lovingly parted—put up a satellite dish so we could watch the goings-on. Having lived and breathed for O.J., I was anxious to involve myself with the current coast-to-coast disgrace. I was just about finished with my latest project and was turned so far into myself and my own doings that I formed concentric circles. I had lived away from Ohio for twenty years. First I was a mother and newspaper columnist in gargantuan Los Angeles, then I was a ghost of my former self in northern Nevada.

My parents had seemed fine when I'd left them. They'd been taking care of their own mothers, Grandma Ethel in Heritage House and Nana at the Park Towers. They were *them,* Mom and Dad: a fully functioning unit. They had each other. They didn't need anyone else. When they reached their seventies, I came to envy them.

I was in my forties, and my parents had a better social life than I did. Every time we spoke, they were going here or there, or they had just come back from Thus-and-So's and had invited Thus-and-So over for drinks the next week.

Often I'd get the answering machine. My dad recorded a different greeting every day. He'd drawl like a cowboy or pretend to be a tall, fey butler. "Helloooo," I'd hear. "The Greeeeeeenneeessss are outttt, but dooo leeeeave a messashhhaaaaahhggee."

This was after Mom's recovery from open-heart surgery. They were hale if not hearty. A few months before the call—the one you're both never and always expecting—I'd spent a few days with them in Florida. My father had slept in his chair most of the time. He'd sat in the sun on the lawn, near the condo, not able to make it to the beach.

In the mornings, when I woke up there, I would lie quietly just to hear the sounds of their voices together. Through the walls of the guest room, with the door closed, I could hear the muffled melody I'd been listening to all my life.

MY MOTHER DEFINED that call in a paper she wrote her freshman year at Wellesley, after her father had died. He was fifty-two. The assignment was to write a story in the third person. My mother got an A.

> Phyllis lay perfectly still while the noise of the phone resounded up and down the hall of closed doors. She thought about the telegram she had gotten every morning that said, "Daddy about the same. We are all fine. Will wire or call if anything new develops."
>
> She closed her eyes again and told herself it was not Mother. Daddy was still living.

I know that "fine" now. It has invisible quotation marks around it.

"How are you?" people ask, and I say "Quotation marks fine."

"How's your mom?" they ask with love and concern.

"Oh, she's quotation marks great," I tell them. "We are both doing quotation marks great."

Phyllis's roommate Peggy threw the door open. "It's for you," she said almost disagreeably. Instinctively, Phyllis asked, "Long distance?"

"Columbus," Peggy grunted. Phyllis ran to the phone with one slipper on and no robe. Across the thousand miles, her mother said very clearly, "I think you had better come home. Daddy had another bad attack." Her mother's voice was steady. Phyllis's hands on the phone were hot and sticky. Her mother was saying, "Take the three-twenty train from Boston. Have one of the girls go in with you. You had better bring along your black dress."

I WAS IN bed for the call. It was very early on a Sunday morning, Pacific Standard Time. The phone rang, and it was my mother, Eastern Standard Time. Long distance compounds physical distance—there was always a time warp when we talked. She said I should come home now. She said, "Daddy thinks you should come home now."

"Like this minute?"

"Like twenty-four hours," she said. "Daddy says."

Within fourteen hours, I was down the mountain and home in Columbus, Ohio, where the airport is quiet—unlike Reno's, where jingling slot machines add to the cacophony.

I took a cab to my parents' house, the first time in

my life I had done so. In all the years I had flown
into Port Columbus, they had been there to pick me
up. These rides home from the airport had become
more and more treacherous as my father got older.
He almost took out a deer on one trip, and another
time, he chose his own turning lane, narrowly es-
caping a collision in his dark green Cadillac. But my
dad wasn't driving anywhere, anymore.

When I arrived at their house, he was in his leather
Eames-like chair in the sitting room. My mother sat
beside him in her chair, a smaller version of his.
Later, she began sitting in his chair. She says it still
smells like him.

I put the files and projects that had been so press-
ing in Nevada in the closet in "my" room across the
hall. Now my mom's home office, it had been my
room while I dawdled at Ohio State. My dad hadn't
let me hang up my renegade TIRED OF THE SAME
OLD SHIT? poster. They had just moved to this house
from our childhood home and were proud of its
seventies no-kids cool. I thought I fooled him when
I hung the poster behind a bookshelf inside the
closet where I was now placing my briefcase. Now
back, I would sleep in this room and get some work
done, I hoped.

By the time I went back to Nevada at the end of
this initial visit, the writing project I had been working on, a book proposal, was in the mail, and my dad

was bedridden. He never got out of that bed again. He stayed there until the December night he died.

That night my mother and I drank tea in the kitchen. I emptied the wastebaskets. We tried to get a little sleep, then began to make our calls.

WE DESIGNATED DAUGHTERS don't come into our roles knowing what to do or how to do it. I knew I was supposed to be strong, but I felt doubtful and fragile. I didn't trust myself to do the job. And what exactly *was* the job? I had already exhaled. I was off duty. My daughter was raised and well on her way. I was walking along, singing a song, perimenopausal, when my mother called. Just as I was getting my sea legs as a relatively carefree woman, I found myself back on my parents' doorstep.

Designated Daughterhood is a contract we do not enter into lightly. We know we're in it for the long run. There is a sadly apt sign at the entrance to my mother's subdivision. NO EXIT, it says.

When my mother said they needed me in Ohio— I'm not sure if she used the word "need," but that was the word I responded to—I couldn't think of a reason they would. I am not the obvious choice, but I am the only choice. I am a daughter born between two sons. There are exceptions, certainly, but the daughter is usually the go-to gal in times of family crisis. Though I'm the daughter, I had never come instantly to mind when any kind of help was needed. My life was art, not responsibility.

I can run a house, sort of, but not in the proper, orderly manner of my parents. I am a lifetime of denim, while my mother is full-blooded Talbots. I do things scattershot, she does things nicely. At one point she tried to convince me that I could save my marriage if I bought a house in San Marino, California, and wore a Talbots suit. Despite evidence to the contrary, I think she still secretly believes it. I cannot put a meal together. I don't even eat meals. I fed my daughter a baked potato for dinner every night from junior high through high school. Not a baked potato as a side dish—a baked potato, that was it. When my mother called, I considered myself across-the-board inept.

I asked the man I was with why my parents would need me. What would I bring to the table?

"Fresh air," he said.

STAYING AT YOUR parents' house, however temporarily, is to be a well-meaning yet squeaky third wheel. You think your squeak is silent, but it's not, and there is no WD-40 to grease the daily differences. Your parents have their routines and rituals, and you have formed your own. They don't use the Land O Lakes nonfat half-and-half that gets you up in the morning. They make one banana last for three days. They don't buy Charmin Ultra, for God's sake. Their sitting room fits two: them. You crouch on an ottoman in the corner, interrupting.

Dad was usually sitting up in bed when I awoke each day and went from my room to theirs at the end of the hall. He had already had his first cup of coffee. Sometimes he'd ask for "more coff," and my mother or I would go down to the kitchen. I still say it in the morning—"More coff?"—to my little Papillon dog, Lausche.

Lately I've put in a new twist.

"Michael Isikoff, Lausche?" I'll say, citing the noted reporter. "Michael Isikoff yet?" I'll ask, and she'll run—I'll shuffle in slippers—to Mr. Coff.

Going for Dad's coff, I'd walk down the hallway, mirrored on one side and carpeted, I swear, in lime-go-go-green. I'd enter the white and turquoise kitchen, designed with a hand-painted cornice featuring watercolor paintings of fruit. A pineapple. A pear. Some light green Granny Smith apples. In the kitchen is a round glass table I've never liked; it's too harsh and cold. My mother keeps it covered with a tablecloth and matching cloth napkins. Always matching napkins. God forbid we should go eclectic and mix patterns in this by-the-book household. When she and I ate together by candlelight at that table during those long months, we'd listen for Dad down the hall. He'd ring a bell if he needed us, but if I was

the one who arrived at the bedroom door, he'd un-
failingly ask for Mother.

I'd walk back into their room with coff to begin
the day. The hallway, the sitting room, their bedroom, "my" bedroom, and the kitchen: Those were
the borders, and this was our bunker. Our world was
father, mother, daughter. Then us and hospice.

I HAVE NEVER minded standing at a sink, loading a
dishwasher, at the end of the day. I like the feeling of
a task completed. I hope the sound at the moment
I die will be of a dishwasher swishing on.

Not far into my first visit home, during a blue-
skied Indian summer, I stood at the sink one morning wearing jean shorts and Weejuns and finally
understood why I was needed in this house: I could
keep the sink free of dishes. It could be the thing I
was counted on to do. My mother would never have
to worry about loading and unloading again. She
could sit with Dad while I did the dishes. I let the
water run warm on my hands and smiled as I lazily
considered this. I looked at the wall behind the sink,
where there was no window, and stared at the bot-
toms of frying pans hung on hooks made to look like
chickens.

When I turned off the water, I heard my mother's
voice coming down a long tunnel, as if she were
calling for help from a frigid cave. Her voice was

strangulated, high and wavering, as it made its way down the hall. "Debby! Debby!" (My mother doesn't call me D.G. except in public, when she thinks it might matter.) "Come help me, Daddy's . . ." I was in their bathroom to hear her say the last word: "fallen."

"Daddy's fallen! Call the squad!" (In Columbus, in a crisis, it's always "the squad.")

I quickly called 911 as I looked on this anguished *Pietà*. Mom's expression was ashamed; she was clearly shocked that she hadn't been able to help Daddy. "Pitched" was the word she used. She'd thought she could get Daddy to the bathroom by herself, but he had pitched toward the shower and gone down. Daddy looked up at me from his wedged position between the toilet and the shower. He smiled and tried to shrug. He was realizing, perhaps for the first time, that imposition was all his body had to offer.

The phone rang. It was a firecracker going off in the bedroom, so charged were we in the panicky bathroom. I bolted to answer it. Couldn't the EMTs find our house? Instead, it was Lois, my mother's friend since 1919, when they both were born.

"Is this a good time?" Lois asked from her house down the road.

"No, this is not a good time, Lois!" I told her. "We're waiting for the squad!" I hung up the phone without explaining and left Lois to her apoplexy. My mom called her back after things had settled down.

My father had pitched, she told Lois, using that word again, the only one that could possibly explain how Daddy could have fallen from her grasp. Then he was safely back in his bed, having been checked out and lifted by strong, calm medics in dark blue uniforms.

I FLEW BACK and forth from Nevada to Ohio that fall and winter. On one trip, the airline couldn't turn down the heat, so we were strangers seated in a scary midair sauna. Another flight was terrifyingly turbulent, so much so that my seatmate and I held hands. She, too, was a Designated Daughter. We introduced ourselves, and our hearts said, "Hello. My parents are sick, old, and dying, and I'm acting like I can hold everything together."

My mother and I had become combat buddies. It was hard for me to leave Ohio each time, and hard for her to watch me go. Back on the Nevada mountaintop, I'd call at five P.M. my time, eight P.M. her time, to see how the day had gone. My body was in the ghost town where I lived, but my soul was in the sitting room chair beside my mom. In a symbol of solidarity, I had bought us matching gray velour pullover robes, which made us look like mouse monks. A drab and silly sight, we took to calling ourselves Jean and Christine, the names of the women who had looked after Nana.

I had not wanted to leave Columbus all those years ago when my former husband, John, had been offered a job in Los Angeles. Our daughter, Maggie, was in kindergarten, and I was going to the Columbus College of Art & Design at night, working at being an artist as well as a mother. We lived in a small red house, painted HGTV-style with yellow accents and green shutters. It had a front stoop and a leafy backyard and curtains in the garage. An army couple had bought it to flip, and we Fulfords were happy there. Even the lavatory wastebasket was covered in matching lavatory wallpaper.

I suppose I always assumed I would be married and have children, but as a little girl, my maternal instinct centered on stuffed animals and my family's dogs and cats.

Maggie was the first baby I ever held. I was captivated by her but characteristically unsure of myself as a mother. I didn't trust myself then. I found myself discussing everything with Maggie, even when she was an infant. I spoke to her as if she were an adult, and shopkeepers called me on it. "You talk to that baby like she is six years old," said one, while five-month-old Maggie and I picked out blue glass bookends for Mom's birthday.

Maggie said "hi" at seven months, not that I'm bragging thirty-two years later. This would startle people riding up an escalator behind us; they'd jump when the hairless head looking over my shoulder spoke.

"I want to grow up and be a mommy and have long, beautiful hair and say 'dammit,'" Maggie told me in our little red house in Columbus. She was my shotgun rider in a Big Bird hat. She was my side-kick.

"If you want to go roller-skating with Cher, you go roller-skating with Cher," I melodramatically said to my husband when he told me about the opportunity to move across the country. *People* magazine had launched a few years earlier, so if Cher was roller-skating, I knew it. I had a tabloid mind even then.

The company courting John flew us out to Los Angeles to look at houses. I could not imagine our midwestern selves surviving in glitter and glam. I did not have an adventurous bone in my body and hated the thought of leaving my parents and friends. I would cry in the backseat of our California real estate agent's car. My Valium was stolen from our hotel room. Then one day we found our home in Altadena, a town up against the San Gabriel Mountains. I had never even seen a mountain before. Seventeen years, a divorce and a daughter grown, a career and a lifetime later, I moved to legendary Virginia City, Nevada. Eventually, I stopped considering ever moving back to Columbus. It was a nice place to visit, you know?

IN THE THREE months leading up to my father's death, my brothers, Bob and Tim, would fly in when they could, one from Chicago, the other from Colorado. They both had families and obligations, and knowing I was around made them feel better about the health and welfare of our parents. They understood that they were on call. Permanently. I did not feel the least bit resentful that the duty was not divided in perfect triplicate. I liked being the know-it-all, reporting how it *really* was at home. One weekend when my brothers were in Columbus, we met with Dr. Shell, who had taken care of my grandmother when he was a young doctor and, as a result, inherited us. That Saturday morning in our parents' living room, Dr. Shell sat on the white couch with the framed pastel portraits of the three of us as children hanging above. He told us, brothers and sister, what we already knew. Our father's body had been ravaged by diabetes for over forty years. Now he was eighty-three, and the nerves in his spine were being strangled by stenosis. It would not be long.

Dad didn't want any visitors. He didn't want to see himself in another's eyes as being in any way diminished. One neighbor came by to visit, a lovely gesture, and I practically chased him down the hall with a hatchet. Mom and I became security guards, talking to friends at the front door while not inviting them in. Visiting nurses would come from the hospital three times a week to bathe Dad, get him into clean pajamas, and turn him in bed. Then we started interviewing men who could lift him, to tend to his personal needs. We went on instinct and referrals; the sick keep an eye on the sick around here, and a good caregiver is as precious as a good babysitter used to be. An accordion player arrived. He had cared for a man a few blocks away who enjoyed music in the night when he couldn't sleep. This musician, in white cowboy boots, came highly recommended by the new widow, who, as it turned out, was deaf. We thanked him very much, and I walked him to the door. We also fired the hulking physical therapist who was too rough with Daddy. Dad called him *Holzhacker*, reaching far back into his generational vocabulary for the word "lumberjack" in German. We had no energy for artifice. The mannerly era in my parents' household officially ended in November when the impeachment hearings began. Even though we turned down the sound on the TV, the words "oral sex" entered the sitting room, where we sat talking to Andre, the genial, diligent, cologne-wearing man we eventually hired to help Dad.

Fast on the heels of the sex talk on TV came swearing. I'd begun to feel comfortable enough to throw a "fuck" or a "shit" around the house. I cussed a lot in my real life and saw no reason to censor myself in this raw moment. My father was trapped in his body, my mother was trapped helping him, hurting, and I was trapped in sadness and frustration, within the narrow bounds of a lime-green hallway. I had come from the Wild West to wade deep into the Midwest, waiting with my mother for my father to die.

My proper Talbots mother let it slip that she and Daddy used to cuss behind closed doors—she and Daddy, from whom we occasionally heard a "goddamn" or a "good goddamn" during our youth.

Mom had been compulsively cleaning closets; she couldn't sit still except when she was in the bedroom with Daddy. She was organizing drawers, going through old files, stopping up a shredding machine that she had treated herself to at Staples. I suggested she give it a rest. The worn-out sheets in the linen closet had been there for thirty-five years. They could wait a while. "Take a load off, Mom," I said.

She laughed hard. "Sometimes Daddy would get so aggravated with me—I'd be doing three things at once, and it used to drive him crazy. He'd say, 'Phyllis, if you stick a broom up your ass, you could sweep the kitchen.' "

My mouth flew open and froze there.

"If you don't look out, your face will freeze that way," Nana said in my head.

My eyes became cartoon spinning eyes. My mom was bent over sideways in Daddy's chair, crying, laughing.

DURING OUR DAYS on death's threshold, people brought us things to eat. Pasta casserole, mushroom soup, chicken paprikash. After one High Holy Day, my cousin Kathy showed up at the door with plastic containers of brisket, kugel, and other ancestral delights. That day, on the front stoop of my parents' house, with the leaves turning color and my cousin's casseroles in my hands, it dawned on me that life didn't have to be as difficult as I'd made it. I had a support system, and it was in this town. I belonged back here, with family. I belonged back here with Mom.

"YOU HAVE TO move here," my older brother said to me one day under his breath. He thought he was hypnotizing me, in the stealthy, lasered way he said it. A silent dog whistle. A voice in your head in a dream. My older brother has always been able to get his message across to me. He's the first person I learned to communicate with—the first letters I could write were BBY, trying to spell his name. I ran around the neighborhood behind him when he had a two-wheeler and I didn't. He once told me "Weejun" was spelled "Ouigian," and I believed him.

"You have to move here," vibrated Bobby.

"No shit," I transmitted to my brother, the swami.

That October, I flew back to the mountain just in time for the Nevada Day Parade, which consisted of twenty drunks and a Model T. I had moved there three years earlier, when the riots and fires and fury that were Los Angeles had become too much to bear. Then, my friend Leon was murdered in his own garage after attending a Clippers basketball game. Los Angeles had become unholy for me. Maggie was off at college; I'd left my job as a newspaper columnist and couldn't afford to live in California anymore. I found Virginia City. It was like living in a pretend town. Fewer than than nine hundred residents were here on the Comstock Lode, a once booming silver-mining territory over 6,300 feet above sea level. Riches from Virginia City built San Francisco and funded the Civil War. Now the town advertises that it is open year 'round.

This fallen boomtown called to me, with its authentic wooden sidewalks and tiers of ramshackle houses climbing up Sun Mountain. I wanted a slowed life so badly. I imagined this ghost town would be the western equivalent of idyllic Martha's Vineyard, where my childhood friend Marcia now lived. While checking out Virginia City, I went to St. Mary's Church to light a candle for Leon. I prayed for a reason to move to the mountain. The entire town was on the National Register of Historic Places, and looked its age, I might add. I woke up with a thought. "Historic town" means "family history." I could teach people to tell their stories here. This was Storey County, after all. I could hear train whistles, church bells, and wind chimes. I prayed for a house with a shop, and a house with a shop appeared.

I saw myself as an evangelist of family history. I planned to give my sermons in the bookstore I opened in the shop I had prayed for, attached to the house. It had been a one-chair beauty salon. The former owner took the chair but left the sink.

My first day of business was Historic Day in May, a big deal in my historic town, also known for its chili cook-offs, mountain oyster festivals (deep fried bull testicles), and camel races. Historic Day had some gravitas to it. A Victorian house across the street was on the tour, and I knew that it would be a popular draw. I didn't want all the hordes from that stop to rush up the steps to my house instead of walking around to the shop. I barricaded the entrance to the house with boxes of books, and I went to the shop, ready to greet customers. I wore a red dress I had ordered from a catalog and Nana's silver watch, engraved with her initials. I had practiced using the cash register and the credit-card swiper. I stayed in the shop with a smile on my face from nine A.M.

until the sun went behind the mountain. I sold one book that day. I got the money wrong three times before the son of my lone customer figured it out for me. I was ashamed of myself. When my loved ones called to inquire how it had gone, I could not lift my voice above a crying croak. I told them I had no sense of humor about this, so just please, no jokes.

A few days after Dad pitched, I could hear Mom on the phone with Lois, saying, "Yes, it's too bad that Debby has to leave now, but she'll be back. After all, she has a whole life in Nevada . . ."

I was sitting in the sitting room, listening.

No, I don't, I thought.

I KNEW WHAT I had to do. I had to get back home to Columbus. Since the silver-mining days in the 1800s, Virginia City had been a spot for dreamers. You could find crystals everywhere, just by glancing at the ground. I was enamored at first, enchanted, but became less so after three years of shopping at Uncle Patrick's Outpost, where Uncle Patrick slept by the register and the Band-Aid boxes and soup cans were dusty. Not a lot of dreamers came along looking to buy ghost-town real estate at the beginning of the millennium, but I went ahead and put the house on the market. Frances, the Realtor who helped me get up the mountain, was going to get me down.

I arrived back in Ohio and began what I think
of as the saddest house hunt in the world. My dad,
dying; my mother, sitting in the bedroom with him,
the answer to his every question. "We're in our bedroom, Bob. Just like we always are. I'm here beside
you, honey, just like I always am."

Each morning I'd run out of my parents' house,
wearing a new brown winter coat. I'd bought it at the
mall in Reno. I'd hop in the car with my Columbus
Realtor, a dear friend—another Lois—who had grown
up across the street from me here in town. Her real
estate partner, Mary Kay, was with her. Her phone
message said, "Don't delay. Call Mary Kay!," which
added to my sense of urgency. Every afternoon I'd
come back in my parents' door, and there they would
be, down that sad hallway, anxious to hear what had
happened, even though my father was at the point
where he really didn't understand. I felt I wasn't being picky, but I looked at 168 houses. It wasn't until
the day my mother agreed to leave Dad's side for
an hour that we walked into an interesting house
together. "Now, *this* is a house," she said, and having
been given the nod, I quickly made up my mind.

That brown coat bundled me in feelings of anxi-
ety and grief and not knowing. I still wear it—it's a
good-looking coat, even with this much mileage on
it. When I've pulled it on again each winter since,
it's as heavy as if I've gone swimming in it. There was

no joy in that house hunt. No happy anticipation. I was leaving the creative isolation and independence I craved and needed. I was moving home, where winter was coming and the only thing I knew was that I would soon be grieving my dad.

Every night I'd take a bath, light a candle, gulp Rescue Remedy, and pray that the house in the ghost town would sell. After living there three years, I knew some solitary iconoclast would have to come along. In the general population, they're in short supply. You have to be a true believer to go to the mountains. How many people were left whose beliefs hadn't dimmed by now?

In our countless hours sitting in the sitting room, my mom listened to my worried obsessions. Tim gave me impeccable real estate advice, while Bob offered assurance that he would help in any negotiations.

"I'll just bet," Mom said, "there is someone who has been driving past that house, wanting it." This even though she'd visited me there, up in the thin air, and kept her disapproving comments to herself. I'd sigh and take baths and worry, and she would just know.

Then one evening, six weeks later, Frances, the Realtor, called and asked if I was ready to put the house under contract with the postmistress and her family, who had wanted the house when I bought it. They had been driving by it all these years.

Naturally, there were complications, and they all had to do with money. I walked into the kitchen one day, and my mother had been on the phone arguing on my behalf with Frances. Frances was asking if it would be okay for the buyers to put in a door between the house and the shop before they'd sign the contract, and, oh yes, there was a ten-thousand-dollar discrepancy in the appraisal calculations—ten thousand that I'd have to eat. Mom was standing in the kitchen, steaming. She'd been taking care of Dad all day and hated it when the phone rang and woke him. She repeated the conversation to me in my brown coat. "I felt like saying to her, 'Go fuck yourself, Frances.'"

I folded in half laughing and saw my mother, my ally, beside me in whatever life was about to give us, and whatever it was bound to take away.

WHEN HER DADDY felt that we needed to send for Debby, he was taking charge of the future as best he could, because he really had no control of the future at all. He wanted her close by, for his own peace of mind—and to support me. That there would be a title associated with her role never would have entered his mind.

He expected death to be more imminent. It was probably only a few weeks after Debby came, and when both of the boys were here, that he lay back to take a nap in the hospital bed that had replaced his in our bedroom. He could not believe that he was alive when he awoke. It was unfair to him that he was.

In those early weeks, when Debby was just visiting, before the brown-coated house search had begun, I was always relieved and happy when she arrived but not really upset when she left. I knew that soon she would return and in the meantime, Bob and I would resume our fifty-six-year privileged, private, one-on-one relationship. We had had an empty nest for a long time, and we had our routines.

My mother had told me more than once that she would never live with me, that it was a recipe for disaster. It surely would have been true for her and me, and I thought it would be true for Debby and me as well. I knew, too, that I would not want my quiet household disrupted both by death and by a daughter at home. It has dawned on me only very recently that my mother's adamant declaration was the result of my father's mother having lived with us for the last year of her life. In those days, the widowed mother moved in with a child, usually a daughter, when available. In our family, my mother—the daughter-in-law—got the duty. It was not a happy year, and although I was only five years old, I remember snippets of the unhappiness of both women involved. At this moment I feel more sympathy for my grandmother than my mother.

Debby and I have never had any unpleasantness between us, even through her teenage years (well, her hair and her choice of clothes, maybe, and a few of the nonconformist boys she chose). At the most basic level, we have the same core values, the same take on things and people. I believe we love each other unconditionally and truly understand each other. It seems obvious to those who meet us, and long-time friends as well, that we are of a similar mind and joined at the soul.

If you know us only superficially, it could be hard to believe that we are so compatible: by the tempo with which we start our day to the way we think of meals and table settings and appropriate attire. We are not mirror images. Debby is sharp, witty, and with it, fun to be with, creative, and a believer in dreams and dream books. She is sociable when she feels like it, but she often pretends that she is invisible in public. I, at her age, really liked being with people and enjoyed all the projects I worked on and those with whom I worked. It is stimulating to me to run into acquaintances at the grocery and have a short conversation. Debby changes aisles to avoid such encounters. I may be too practical; I do not know the signs of the zodiac and find little difference between astrology and atrophy. She believes in horoscopes and symbols; I call some of her nostrums and remedies "voodoo" medicine. She is a Taurus. I am a Post (Emily).

Her visits during Bob's illness were a godsend; the time we spent together as this journey began was a confirmation that we were on the same wavelength, that the mother/daughter relationship was more nearly a friendship of contemporaries. Debby lightened my load, physically, mentally, and spiritually. Bob was leaning on me, but I was leaning on her. What a backpack of worries she shouldered. We had moments of laughter and despair and of increasing harmony. I marveled at her sensibilities as she connected with the hospice nurse, understood how Bob was thinking about a funeral—not his but his father's—and brought an oil painting of Grandpa Nick into the room, found the prayer book, and held a ceremony in front of his bed.

I cannot even remember when Debby first told me that she was moving home for good. I must have been too overjoyed to note the time or the place or the medium. Did she call? Was it on one of the fly-ins? All I knew was that we would be under the same Ohio sky, in the same Ohio city, each in a home of our own.

She assured me, and reassured me, that she wasn't making the move only for me, that it was also for her. I assured her, and reassured her, that I would be all right alone. I thought that I could probably manage on my own. But I could feel the loneliness beginning to seep in, even though I had friends and activities and two very attentive long-distance sons. After twenty years, Debby was ready for home. I wanted to believe that, and, having seen her ghost town in Nevada, I did. And I was more than ready to have her come back.

Now I would have a sympathetic ear and a hand to hold and my daughter, designated the day she was born, to be my next life's companion.

3

THE MERGE

Y FATHER DIED in the night. My mother came into my room to tell me. She couldn't be sure, but she thought so, she said.

I couldn't be sure, either. We talked to Dad, asked him if he could hear us. This is common among families, I'm told. The mind is unable to absorb what has happened. We held a mirror up to Dad's mouth. We listened to his chest and tickled his feet. Finally, Mom kissed him on the lips, and he did not respond. We knew then to call the hospice nurse, who washed him and dressed him in clean blue pajamas. The funeral home sent a team who zipped his body up in a black rubber bag and carted him away.

He never left that house, though. Everything is "Daddy this" or "Daddy that" or "Daddy used to say." Mom and I do not live in a vacuum, even though we felt the most comfortable that way in the first years after Dad's death. We formed our own world, but we were not alone in it. Bob and Tim (and Dad) sat with us in Mom's sitting room. We are a family who knows one another's reactions and idiosyncrasies, and Mom and I discuss them constantly, repeating old jokes and phrases. Although my brothers come to Columbus and then go, they are in constant contact on the phone. Through Mom, each of us knows what the other is up to every single day.

I REMEMBER THOSE first winter days, bright white sunshine coming through the window. My mother sat at the end of her dining room table, writing thank-you note after thank-you note, facing the kitchen, not the yard. Her dining room table. Their dining room table. Her house. Their house. I don't know when we made the verbal switch.

It would be a month or so until I moved into the house I bought in my brown coat. It took a dreary month for Mom, my brothers, and me to settle deathy things. I became her powerful attorney—of course it's power of attorney, I know it's power of attorney, I just amuse myself and annoy others this way— because I'd be living in Ohio. We wearily and tearily began the process of readjusting, sending copies of certificates to the entities that required them. A local reporter called. He wanted to do a story about Dad, who was a well-known businessman in town, so my older brother spoke to him. The article appeared after Bob went back to Chicago. My mother called to read him the story on the phone. Suddenly, she was laughing as hard as I'd ever seen her laugh; she was laughing like she used to laugh with Dad.

Poor reporter. He had gotten his facts and anecdotes absurdly mixed up. My dad used to have lunch with his friends downtown at the same place every day. This was when Dad worked downtown. This was when Dad was a young man. He'd walk to lunch from his office. My mother read the paper to my brother in spasms, laughing until she couldn't get the words out.

What the reporter wrote, bless his heart, and what the readers read, was that my dad, until the day he died, walked fifteen miles downtown for lunch. My dad, my sick, old, paralyzed, bedridden dad.

MY FATHER USED to call them soup carriers, the good-hearted people who brought food to the bereaved. My mother, to this day, uses Dad language: "Soup carriers," she'd say when a casserole came, using words to keep him alive.

Soup carrying is a tradition in every culture. Friends feed the mourners until they can stand up after loss. Each community has its own way of doing it. In ours, someone is always assigned to the food, to mark platters for return to their owners, to let people know what they can bring. Someone keeps the pastry boxes bunched together by the phone and the cold cuts in top-of-the-line zip-up plastic bags. To put the mayonnaise back in the refrigerator. To wrap in cellophane and record who brought what. These are the days after death.

My mother uses a filing-card system passed down from widow to widow, generation to generation, in Columbus, Ohio. Hieroglyphics of grief. The friends are alphabetically ordered on index cards inside a file box. I was dispensed to Staples to pick up these supplies. As each further kindness comes in, it is duly noted on the donor's card. It is hard to remember even kindnesses when your world lies disassembled.

My mother sat with her file box for hours, writing to people on beautiful note cards we ordered for the occasion. We chose off-white card stock with forest-green ink. We put a poem by John Updike on it. We thought he would understand.

> *And another regrettable thing about death*
> *Is the ceasing of your own brand of magic,*
> *Which took a whole life to develop and market—*
> *The quips, the witticisms, the slant*
> *Adjusted to a few, those loved ones nearest*

The lip of the stage, their soft faces blanched
In the footlight glow, their laughter close to tears,
Their tears confused with their diamond earrings,
Their warm pooled breath in and out with your heartbeat,
Their response and your performance twinned.
The jokes over the phone. The memories packed in the rapid-
    access file. The whole act.
Who will do it again? That's it: no one;
Imitators and descendants aren't the same.

My mother had clipped the poem from *The New
Yorker* years ago and kept it in a manila file folder.
Dad bronzed baby shoes for a living, but he was born
to be an actor. Updike's words were perfect—Daddy
on the stage, us in the audience, Mom in diamond
earrings, applauding, knowing he could never be
replaced. And there I was, not trying to replace him,
exactly, but filling up the empty space he'd left beside my mother. She was nearing eighty at the time
and healthy, except for her heart condition—both
the medical and broken parts. We use euphemisms.
She was "tippy" in her gait. That was not hard to di-
agnose. She was trying to regain her balance, having
lost half of herself.

I had my own subconscious motives for sticking
around.

I would get my mommy to myself.

When Dad was alive, you didn't get that much of

Mom. Dad needed a lot of attention. Growing up, I had to share her with Bobby and Timmy. We were a busy family in a station wagon, and then suddenly we were all kind of old and gone. At fifty, I was home to hear the voice that had always sounded in my head. At fifty, I would quiet down and listen.

Mom and I are practically conjoined now, in accordance on most of the big things and tolerant of most of the small. But we are—and always have been—an odd couple, with diametrically opposed vibes. I have a photograph that tells the story instantly: My mom and I stand in front of the red house in Columbus where I lived with my former husband and our daughter. I was about twenty-eight, an adult, but one with her head in the clouds. My mother—called "Wede" by Maggie and all grandchildren ever after—had stopped by after getting a prestigious civic-volunteerism award from the mayor. She was wearing it around her neck, the gold medal on lustrous red-white-and-blue draped ribbon. In the photo, she has on a blue-and-white seersucker suit with a red geranium corsage. She holds her purse. I am next to her. Somewhere at my feet, my bare feet, is a longneck Bud Light. I point to myself, miming, Why didn't *I* get the award? I have on a sleeveless undershirt, a necklace of charms and amulets, and stringy cutoff blue jeans. I love this picture because in it, my mom looks like *she's* proud of *me*.

In the twenty years after that picture was taken, I moved to California with my family, started a career that sustained me, got divorced, wrote books, moved to a ghost town, ran a bookstore, and whittled down my existence until I hardly recognized myself. By the time I returned to Columbus, I was used to autonomy, and I liked it. I hoped my quirky eccentricities would not jolt my mother's time-honored standards.

My mother wears pearls on Sunday afternoons.

My mother wears stockings on a plane.

What would this renewed relationship be like? We have led divergent lives. My mother is a pillar of the community. I am, in the words of a babysitter who watched my daughter, more of a *bohème*. Would we, as adult women, comfortably merge in Columbus, Ohio? We had been foxhole buddies, sure, but would our growing symbiosis stick?

OUR FIRST VISITS to the cemetery were wrenching. Now we find them consoling. I'd even say I enjoy them, the same way I enjoy a big cry. Since Green Lawn is large, the oldest cemetery in Columbus, it can be difficult to find where you're going, particularly when muted by grief. The cemetery people try to make it easy for mourners by painting different-colored stripes on the road. To get to Dad, you follow white to red and turn where red merges with yellow. You learn your landmarks. Dad lies across from a field of soldiers, which we knew would make him happy. There's a big rock, and a tree stump, and in the distance a stone that says HANNAH.

"Turn left at Harvey Cashatt," Lois used to tell us. Lois's parents and grandparents are there. She enjoyed going, too. Everyone is connected in this section of the cemetery, all the Jewish families of early Columbus. We are embroidered among them. This leafy spot is the true foundation of a community that lived together, married each other, and buried each other for centuries. All the names are familiar. An afterlife *Cheers*.

My friend Patti, who is living with her widowed mother, visits her father's grave site, too. Her mother bought four figurines, one for each season, to leave on her husband's grave. One by one, they disappeared. Patti's mother got angry. On Father's Day, Patti heard a strange tap—tap—tap. When she turned to look, she saw her mother hammering a sign into the ground, warning any would-be thieves that if they stole another figurine, they would be fined and prosecuted to the full extent of the law.

As Designated Daughters, we have to remind ourselves to play with kids our own age. We can get consumed with our mother, our mother's needs, and our mother's world. Maggie accuses me of acting, at times, as if I'm in my eighties. Peer pressure, I tell her. I know my mother and I can be dangerously

insular, and sometimes it feels like we're living the
same life. At times it is confining. And then I feel
guilty about *that*.

I HAVE CALLED my mother at nine-thirty every
morning since the day I moved into my own house
after Dad died. The calls began as reassurance: "Did
you make it through the night?" When one person is
taken from you, you suspect others might leave in the
dark. Mom and I weren't sleeping well at first, and we
discussed that. Grief has symptoms, like colds do. In
grief, there's exhaustion and confusion; there's nap-
ping. There are viscous tears, thicker than everyday
tears, that come from a well so deep you imagine it
covered in moss.

My grief was different from my mom's grief. Years
in, my mom admitted she opened her curtains many
a morning, looked out, and said, "Oh, shit, Bob.
Another day."

The nine-thirty calls evolved and became a perk
in our relationship. They were editorial meetings,
reporting dreams and aches, and whatever. Each of
us in our own tableau, she in her chair, me in my
bed, where I most often can be found. Morning meeting, morning mass. Breaking-news updates, or what
passes for news.

"Have you read Speed Read yet?" I asked.

Speed Read is the "spoiler" they put inside the

front page of the paper—blurbs to tell you what's inside.

"No, I'm just getting to it," said my mother.

" 'GOP's Lack of Teamwork a Blow to Boehner,' " I told her.

She looked it up and laughed. "It's B-O-E-H-N," she told me.

"I know, but still."

"But still," she said.

"That's it," I said.

On the days I wake up late, I panic and call her before I even get to the bathroom.

"Good morning," she'll say, as she's said every morning for the past eight years. "Hello" is for others. "Good morning" is for me, a secret handshake.

"I just got up! I'll call you, I'll call you!" I freakedly yell, with bladder bursting.

"Take your time, darling," she says.

Another morning: "Have you read your daughter's e-mail?" she asked.

"I'm not there yet," I told her.

Zach was starting preschool for two-year-olds the next week. The preschool was affiliated with a congregation that Maggie and her husband were joining.

"The temple is requesting the date of Daddy's death and Hebrew name," Mom told me.

"Daddy's Hebrew name? Daddy doesn't have a Hebrew name."

"I know." My mom laughed.

"Um, tell Maggie it's Baba Booey," I said.

A pause and coughing. Mom didn't get satellite radio and wouldn't be a Howard Stern fan if she did. "Maggie will get it," I said.

A FEW WEEKS ago Mom asked me to catch her up on the zeitgeist. Her with her interest in politics, me with my *People*-magazine brain.

"I see these names, and I feel so dumb," she said. "I have no idea who these people are."

"Like who?" I asked her. "Cyndi Lauper? Tina Turner?"

There was a time when Maggie was in a Madonna stage, like every ten-year-old girl in America. Wede knew Madonna but didn't know Cyndi from Tina. She used to pronounce Lauper "Leeeowwper," which Mag and I would imitate.

"Like Lindsay Lohan?" I asked.

"Like Lindsay Lohan," she said, "and why do I have to know about her?"

"Oh God, don't feel dumb about not knowing who Lindsay Lohan is. I don't have to know about her, and I know more about her than I know about myself!"

We talk at least three times a day. Sometimes four.

Sometimes more. We talk at nine-thirty and often a few minutes after that, with an obituary alert or birth announcement when one has beaten the other to that page of the paper.

"Did you see that baby named Lexus?" I asked Mom.

"Yes, darling," she said.

We talk the minute we get in from any place, which grates on me a little. When I come in the door, I like to reacclimate. I like to hang up my keys, take off my glasses, check the phone and AOL, pour a Coke Zero, and then sit down to call her. To Mom, each return home is a relief. She likes to hear "safe and sound," if only safe and sound from CVS.

We talk post-*Oprah* and most nights around seven-thirty. Usually, she's heading to her shower and then to her smooth sheets. Usually, I'm in bed already, in my wrinkled magpie's nest with my dog, Lausche, securely surrounded by library books and magazines, catalogs, paper napkins, Kleenexes, two remotes, and the phone.

We plot our course during our morning phone calls (those are her words, not mine). When it was easier for Mom to walk, when she had more energy, I'd think of a day out doing things together in a booming announcer's voice: WHEN ERRANDS COLLIDE.

We had the Bermuda Triangle, of course—Kroger,

CVS, and the library—but we'd branch out to the bird-food store or to Leona the seamstress, to the "big box" stores, to Target, to Lowe's, to Easton, to Bob Evans, Bob Evans, and Bob Evans. We are comfortable companions, never harsh with each other. Mom tries to hide it when she braces herself, thinking I'm turning too wide into traffic, and she never gets mad when I get lost, which is every single time. One day we drove to Target to Kmart to Home Depot to Lowe's, trying to find replacement cushions for her outdoor furniture. After we bought what Lowe's had to offer, we stuffed them into my PT Cruiser along with the old ones we were trying to match. I had just leased this PT Cruiser. It would not start.

On another day, with another companion, this glitch might have made me blow my stack. "Daddy would have gone through the roof," Mom said, and I agreed. With her blessed disposition as a guide, we laughed our way through the annoyance. "We don't care" is an oft-used mantra of ours, and as long as we're together, we don't.

"By the way," Maggie says to me so often, "you don't have to refer to Wede as 'my' mom. I know who you're talking about."

THE STREETS OF Columbus did not run with milk and honey, and my professional life dwindled rapidly.

I am able to let down my armor with Mom. One day when I was feeling particularly loser-ish, I lamented how fearful I felt about not being able to stand on my own two feet.

"You don't have to," my mother told me. "You can stand on my feet. They're the same feet."

"I think you are too hard on yourself," she said one day after we'd been to Nordstrom. "You act like you can't do anything, and you know you are a *most* capable—"

I had to interrupt her. "You are talking to the person who just spent forty-five minutes in a dressing room putting on two pairs of *identical* black pants—*same* size, *same* style—and taking them off again and pulling them on again, attempting to see which fit better. Same pants."

"Oh yeah," she said.

THE VERIZON STORE was on Mom's errand list one day. Her cell phone had frozen, no buttons moving, and the screen-saving picture of a tractor was stuck in the field. We'd hoped to be in and out, we'd hoped for no rigmarole with this transaction, but a cell-phone store, like everything, tends to take much more time than you'd think. The customer-service window was not fully staffed, so they were making us wait. They were making lots of people wait. Mom thought she could talk logic with the manager, an activity she enjoys and usually wins. "Your ads say you want new customers, but how are you going to take care of them when you can't take care of the ones you already have?" she asked pleasantly. I was gazing at cell phones numbly when the customer-service agent finally called out, "Phyllis!"

"We're Phyllis," I answered as Mom and I walked toward the desk from different sides of the room.

I HAD GRIEVED my heart into little shreds for six months. From December 1998 until well into 1999, I tried to contain my hurt inside myself, even though I couldn't fool my children.

And then. I sat down and typed that sorrow and loneliness and, in equal measure, my happy memories into the computer. I wrote and I wrote until, finally, the emotions that had come out through my fingers turned into a book. I thought I had discovered that journaling is the best way to work through grief; of course, that is the advice that all support groups give new widows. And thus, at eighty I became an author.

For most of 2000, I had been me on the outside, a full-fledged octogenarian, but, inside, a whirlpool of creative juices. I was still driving and doing for myself: same old grocery shopping and same old meals, spending time with Debby. Sitting at the computer, trying to make sense of my random maunderings, I realized I was learning to accept the loss of my husband. Not that I had much choice. I was a work in progress with a work in progress.

I continued to do what we widows do: go out to lunch and dinner with one another, go to meetings and card games and concerts. The Bob Evans menu was bookmarked into my brain as I arrived for lunch three times a week. I had one leg still in the past, but the other one was itching to get on with what might lie ahead.

Like the Phyllis of old who had often hand-carried the Christmas gifts to Chicago, I went once again to see our grandson, Nick, star in his junior high school play. He brought down the house. Faculty and parents and we, his family, almost rolled on the floor in laughter. Greene genes were front and center. I saw Bob in every move, not a copy but an inheritance. I was on my way back to normal. To prove it to myself, I went shopping and bought a handsome black silk suit that I am still wearing.

The world almost came to a halt on September 11, 2001. That awful day will be with us always, but even as the miasma settled over us, October 5, 2001, arrived, and my book was in bookstores.

It is pure hubris, I know, to feel so full of yourself. But is it a sin for an eighty-year-old woman to laugh for the sheer joy of laughing when she flies off to the elite East to promote her book, when she talks to Katie and Diane and at the prestigious R. J. Julia bookstore in Madison, Connecticut? When she is technically alone but has a publisher's representative helping her aging persona almost every step of the way?

Later, Debby and I had a few joint local appearances, she with *One Memory at a Time: Inspiration & Advice for Writing Your Family Story;* me with my one memory, *It Must Have Been Moonglow: Reflections on the First Years of Widowhood.* Our morning calls lasted longer than I want to admit. Not only did we have the local (very local) news to relate to each other, but now we had "bidness," too. For our book appearances, should I read first or should she? Would we each talk about a chosen topic, or would we respond to the other's topic? We were feeling our way to professionalism, and we were doing it together. We were partners—a mother and a daughter, yes, but there was a new dimension to the bond that had always existed. She was my willing ear; my secrets were safe with her. She made me secure, and in what had begun to feel like an unfamiliar world, she made me not so alone.

It was all a kind of guilty pleasure. There was the inescapable nagging acknowledgment that none of this would have happened if Bob hadn't died. Was I, in some awful way, dancing on his grave? In reality, Debby and I would go to the cemetery and cry. Debby talked to him out loud; I stood, shaking my head at the enormity of my loss. There is not a

TV studio in the world that I would not have forgone gladly to have had one more good day as a wife. Nor would I have cared if I had never been in a hotel suite or been driven from an airport or had this peek at the larger world. But there I was.

4

GOOD TIMES

HREE YEARS INTO Designated Daughterhood, I begged off for a few days to go to a spa in California with Maggie. At this stage of the game, I was more daughter than mother. Mag was at a crossroads, changing jobs, and I felt I knew a thing or two about that. I was anxious to share some time with her and balance the "am I a mother or am I a daughter" teeter-totter inside me. Our second day there, my uncle Al Harmon called to tell us that Mom had had a heart episode, which is medical code for "scary." It was difficult to give in to deep, aromatic massages after a phone call like that. My brothers had flown in to be with Mom; Al was there, too. Still, I felt the guilt and the pout of my own selfishness. I never get to see my daughter, damn it! I never get to go to a spa!

My mother had been at a spa in Florida with her mother, my nana, when Nana had a heart attack. This was at the same time I got engaged. They had to stay in Florida, in hospitals and hotel rooms, not knowing anyone, until Nana was strong enough to come home. So being at the spa with my daughter and getting a phone call like this . . .

Maggie and I ended up calling the experience Canyon Dungeon.

Until then things had been going gloriously well. Mom and I were out and about, reenergized. The book project I was working on when Dad died became reality, and Mom was busy with *Moonglow*. Our nine-thirty calls became our own mini-writers' colony as we'd encourage and urge each other on. Five o'clock was time for cocktails, and I'd go over to her house for wine and popcorn or wine and dinner, but always for wine.

Mom felt good, and when Mom felt good, I felt good. To know what you have when you have it is key. It is the take-home message of the Bonus Years.

Although I spent so much time with Mom, I was not without friends. All my life, I've been blessed with spectacular girlfriends. I had Jill in Columbus, I had Lindsey, I had Lynn and Diny, I had Sally, I had Amy and Barbara, her twin. I had my cousins Julie, Kathy, and Molly, and my two Marcias, one in

Connecticut, the other on the Vineyard. I had Annie in New Orleans, on the phone. But I'm pretty
much a hermit, so I didn't see a lot of them in the
first few years. Mom's social life became my social
life. I was her date, her escort. My place cards read
"Guest of Phyllis Greene." We went to luncheons and
functions and dinners and lectures. She was fully
mobile, and we had fun.

And what an entrée it was, being Phyllis Greene's
daughter. Eighty-seven years of goodwill. What
trouble she had introducing me, though. I stood
beside her, a comparatively fresh face in a sea of
stooped shoulders, white heads, and shrinking people. My hair was tricolor then—red, blonde, and
brunette—and I usually wore it in a spout on the
top of my head, secured by a plastic hair orna-
ment.

"Whomever, I'd like you to meet our daughter,
D. G. Fulford, Debby Greene," Mom would say.
She tried to acknowledge the professional me but
couldn't help putting me in parentheses to clarify
"(Debby Greene, the real one, the one who grew
up here)." Most people end up calling me D.J.
anyway, and I don't bother to correct them. Mom
continues to say "our daughter." Dad is with us
everywhere we go.

Mom is a one-man woman. Dad has been her only

love. I think if she should get married again, the only man good enough would be Walter Cronkite. I told her this.

She said, "As if."

"As if?" I said.

"As if I'd ever want anyone other than Daddy."

I envy Mom and Dad their in-jokes and intimacy that remain even after he's gone. But sometimes I'm afraid I've become so entwined with my mother that I have no room for another relationship. I did have lunch with a younger guy once, and I remembered to hide my Centrum Silver.

If I am reading my fear correctly, there is another reason I dismiss the thought of pairing up: I don't want to be a widow.

Being a Designated Daughter is close enough.

BEFORE MY MOTHER'S heart episode, she would drink white wine, and I would drink red wine at our nightly cocktail hour.

"Oh, God, Debba," Mom said, using yet another name for me, one that's private and dear. "Am I going to end up an old drunken pirate?" That made me laugh even harder than usual. Eighty-plus years of being perfect, and I was coaxing her over the line. After the heart episode, though, her doctor said she could have only four ounces of wine each day.

"A lousy four ounces" is what we call it.

"A drink, Mrs. Greene?" "Yes, white wine, please, but just give me a lousy four ounces." "Phyl? For you?" "A lousy four ounces of white," she'll say. "Thank you very, very much."

MOM'S EPISODE WAS the fog that came on pit-bull feet. Things go great, and then there is a reminder. There is a reminder that you have signed on for the long run, what a responsibility that is, and what it really means. Spending these years with our aging mothers, we get a hard pinch every once in a while. Time to sit up and pay attention. It's not all lunches and laughs.

I sat in the waiting room at the hospital with my uncle Al when Mom went back in for heart stents. I prepared as if I were up for jury duty and brought a thick book, Milton Glaser's *Art Is Work*. I had legal pads for note-taking in the brocade portfolio that my friend Connecticut Marcia gave me years ago. It has held many a file for me, the first being the paperwork from my mediated divorce.

Of course, I didn't even crack Milton Glaser. I spoke softly, using words like "episode," with my loving uncle. I asked him if there was anything he thought I should be doing differently for Mom.

"Deb, you could run over somebody in a car, and

your mother would say 'Isn't that wonderful?'" he said.

MY COUSIN JULIE was turning fifty. Our family is great for traditions, and one of them is to mark a big to-do in song, such as the ever popular number written for Dad's seventieth birthday, all of us gathered in Florida wearing "Bob Greene is 70" T-shirts on the beach.

To the tune of "New York, New York":

Start spreading the news,
His day is today
We've come to be a part of it
Bob Greene, Bob Greene!

Similar performances were recommended if not required for Julie's birthday. Mom and I decided we'd be the Jewish Judds. We had a somewhat personal relationship with the Judds, we felt. I had written a newspaper column about their 1991 pay-per-view final concert when Naomi left to fight hepatitis and Wynonna struck out alone. The looks that passed from Judd to Judd said even more to me than their music. Everything you want your daughter to know was in there, as well as everything you want to tell your mother.

"I'm scared. I'm sad. Aren't we lucky?"

"I'm so very proud of you."

"Can I do it without you? I wish you could come with me."

"Thanks for everything. I wish we could freeze time."

Naomi saw my column, and we began a correspondence. Mom and Naomi wrote to each other, too, on real stationery, in the days before e-mail. "Wy comes down to my farm every day on her new turquoise Harley-Davidson hog," Naomi wrote. "Ashley, my 23-year-old, got a hiatus from NBC's *Sisters* to star in a small-budget film." She sent me a guardian-angel night-light in a box on which she wrote Psalm 9 in black marker: "For he shall give His angels charge over thee, to keep thee in all thy ways." She added, "Do you know guardian angels are real? We must speak them into action."

For Julie's song, Mom and I wrote new words to the tune of "Mama He's Crazy." We practiced to my *Judds' Greatest Hits* tape on my boom box. Mom started to use the word "boom box," which was more than odd. She usually said "hi-fi."

Julie is a small woman with a high karate ranking, a doctorate, grandchildren, and a cause—the IMPACT Safety program. What rhymes with that? Well, we could throw in some family nicknames, we thought, like Dahmo and Doo. We bought long red wigs and wore killer western shirts I keep in my closet. We brought our boom box with us and took the mike when it was our turn. We sang with tuneless voices but a lot of energy.

To the tune of "Mama He's Crazy":

> *Dahmo, we're crazy,*
> *Crazy 'bout our Doo*
> *Who would know*
> *That we would have*
> *A five-foot fightin' Jew*
> *She got her Ph.D.,*
> *And Dahmo, can't you see?*
> *Dahmo, we're crazy.*
> *Crazy 'bout our Doo.*

ONE NIGHT WE attended a summer party and saw a friend with an indeterminate accent, which is strange, since she was born in Columbus. The accent got more foreign as the night wore on.

"*Und* I said to him," she told us, "I don't want the pink ones *und* the white ones, I only want the pink ones. *Und* he said to me . . ."

"What is with '*und*'?" I finally asked her. *Und* I don't remember her answer. I was still drinking. "Und" is big in our lexicon now. It even begins our phone calls.

"Good morning," Mom says every day.

"*Und?*" I ask.

WE WENT OUT to talk about our books together, like the nice version of Joan and Melissa Rivers. We'd carefully work out what we'd say. "First you'll go, and then I'll go, and then you'll go." Toward the end, we got very cavalier about it. "You do Poplin Suit, then I do Summer Solstice, then you do Popcorn Fart, and then Q and A."

Some venues called for more shtick than others. When Mindy from the temple called, we were ready with the shtickiest.

Mom called me on my cell phone to begin. I pretended I was surprised to hear it ringing as I sat right beside her and dug through my purse for my phone. I opened it up.

"Good Shabbos, D.G.," she said.

"Good Shabbos, Mom," I answered, looking out at the sisterhood, hoping to get a little laugh before we told our stories again.

THERE WAS ONLY one award Mom ever coveted. When she was eighty, she got it: the Julian Sinclair Smith Celebration of Learning Award from the Columbus Metropolitan Library. Our library ranks number one in the country for libraries its size. My mom and I are huge fans. I once spent a college spring vacation holed up in the basement of the library's periodical morgue. I was researching Bob Dylan, not for a paper but for the pure joy of the hunt.

We were all dressed up, taking pictures in the foyer of the library. Mom wore an elegant St. John suit, the first she had rewarded herself with in all her life. I wore a red suit with a beautiful purple velvet burn-out scarf, red suede strappy pumps, my hair blonder, redder, and bigger than ever. Somehow the publisher of the *Columbus Dispatch* got in the family picture of us that ran in the magazine *Columbus Monthly*. I have been calling him "Uncle Mike" ever since, but it's never helped me land a job.

Mom shared the dais with Joyce Carol Oates. Joyce Carol Oates! Mom was shining. It was just like the Updike poem Mom used to describe Daddy, but this time Mom wore her diamond earrings, and she was the one spotlighted onstage.

Our last gig of the year was at Schoedinger's, the downtown funeral chapel. We were asked to participate in a candlelighting ceremony. "To share with others your experiences after the death of a loved one," the funeral director wrote on funeral letterhead. The tribute began at five P.M., in the cheerless gray of early winter—December 7, the anniversary of the attack on Pearl Harbor.

I can't walk into Schoedinger's without crying. I

walk through the heavy door, past the rack you hang your coat on, and I attempt to hold the Pavlovian grief back, but it keeps coming like the hiccups. I cried so much at the funeral of a relative I barely knew that I thought the Schoedinger brothers would have to lift me up under my arms, drag me to the reception room, and give me smelling salts. I think that after the death of a parent, every funeral feels like one of your own.

So we were there, Mom and I, sitting by the candelabra, holding our notes and handkerchiefs. Mom made a face at mine. It was a black bandanna. In the pew where the mourners sat were people who had lost someone during the past year. Some were months removed from their loss, some were weeks, and some were days. I recognized a woman who lit a candle for her daughter, someone I went to high school with who died of breast cancer three days before the ceremony.

Mom began. "For those of you who are veterans, or are mourning the loss of a veteran, this day has special meaning. It does for us. We are here at this lovely memorial service to remember. It is in our memories that we keep truth alive, that we can find our joy still residing—and hiding—in our hearts."

Each funeral or memorial service for me is not only a flashback, it is a prediction. Images enter my mind uninvited.

"My daughter and I share our memories of Bob every day—every day—and she has chosen to read this passage from *One Memory at a Time:* 'Summer Solstice.' "

Mom tossed the floor to me, and I read about seasons bringing back memory, familiar forgotten sounds speeding us back, as do sight, smell, taste, and the feel of a soft old blanket on your skin. I read about my dad, an aficionado of the perfect summer evening.

As I read my own words, my mind was playing its own reading from the High Holy Days memorial service.

"At the blowing of the wind and in the chill of winter, we remember them. At the opening of the buds and in the rebirth of spring, we remember them."

I was a soggy mess when it was our turn to light our candle.

THERE ARE SEASONS in Designated Daughterhood. There is rebirth and rapid change. On that chill day of winter, we'd gone from a vaudeville act to weeping women once again.

⌐

AS D.G. AND I began our days with that oft-mentioned phone call, her primary purpose was to be certain I had made it through the night. My desire, because D.G. is funny, was to have a good laugh.

That was just the first call of the day. When you can and do talk to each other three times a day, there is three times as much to talk about. It is strange that when she was in California and we spoke about once a week, the trivia had become so trivial that it was not worth mentioning.

The multiple phone calls signified the beginning of the good times for me.

My mother told me once that she envied a friend who was an easy laugher. I'm not sure whether I was born with a laughing advantage or if I learned it from Bob, but an early-morning burst of laughter can set the tone for my day.

My spirits were higher than I ever could have hoped at this stage of the game, the game being Widowland. It was not unlike Candyland; you spin the dial and the arrow points the way. The only difference is that in real life, you believe you can control the arrow. But luck plays a large part in both.

My luck was my health and my Columbus support system. My luck was my children.

One of the first times I flew alone that year, I walked through security and then got on a cart that whisked me to my gate. On the way down, the cart driver asked me if I knew that the airport was now charging five dollars for a cart ride, and I said it was news to me but certainly worth it. When I got to my boarding area, early as always, my bag was opened and searched. I had been wanded at security because of my pacemaker, and I had dutifully removed my shoes. What was it about my black suede coat and my matching shoes and purse that said "terrorist profile" to them? Somehow they had gotten it mixed up with "little aging white-haired lady." In the spirit of keeping some sense of self, I asked about the five-dollar charge and found I had been scammed. I was asked to identify the driver, but I said I couldn't. I could have, but I was afraid to. I was not such an independent hotshot after all.

The good times were really beginning. I went to Steamboat Springs to see the United States women's hockey team play an exhibition game against my grandson Tucker's team, the Steamboat Braves, and then I was with them at an after-game party to watch the Super Bowl. What lovely young women they were, and what a gala weekend. From there, I went to visit my Chicago family, then came home to change my clothes and go to Florida to visit my brother and sister-in-law, Al and Sue.

If Florida is pretty close to the center of the geriatric world, Longboat Key might be the epicenter, where the median age is sixty-eight. It made perfect business sense to send me to promote my book where the widows and widowers congregate. With Longboat as my hub, I was sent around the state by limo. What a treat.

We are not unsophisticated in the Heartland, but those limousines are not ubiquitous. You can find them in the Yellow Pages but seldom on the street except at prom time.

So it was almost childish fun to be cruising the Florida

countryside with D.G., who had come down just before Sue and Al went home. Peering out of that car, knowing no one could see in through the tinted windows, we were midwestern to the core, but who, to the people watching, might we be?

Thinking back to 2001, when we went on the book-selling safari, I realize just how good those good times were.

We could no more make a trip like that now than fly me to the moon, and as I sit in the comfort of my own room, I revel in once having thought I was queen of the road.

5

Planes, Trains, Automobiles, and a Wheelchair

N THE SPRING, I found myself look-ing for a mother-of-the-bride dress. My beautiful Maggie was engaged to the wonderful Jon, and their wedding would take place high atop a hill in Los Angeles the following April. Lest you think this threw me into an organiza-tional frenzy, be assured it did not. Maggie and Jon had it handled. Mag tended to every detail, recorded in a hugely fat wedding notebook. She wouldn't take advice from me with a ten-foot pole.

I was to "lead the pack" of the three mothers: me; Cheryl, the wife of my ex-husband, John (and my warm friend), who is very va-va-voom; and Vilia, the groom's mother, who is British and a judge.

"I don't think you want your upper arms to show. I mean, I'm trying to put it gently, but you know?" my daughter said to me in a phone call about the dress. She specifically asked me to look like a mother. I was not surprised at her request; on the last Fourth of July when she and Jon came to town, I had pink hair. I did not have pink hair anymore, and she knew it. Pink had been merely a celebration of summer. I had planned to work my way down from calico cat to tortoiseshell by the time of the wedding.

"Not fluffy, not slinky," Maggie told me. This threw me back to a dressing room, one of the legion we've shared over the years.

"Mom! You're forty! Face it," she said to me in 1998 as I tried on leather pants I thought made me look like rock star Chrissie Hynde, if Chrissie Hynde were really short.

At social occasions, I like to sparkle a bit. A lot. Long, flowing skirts heavy with seed beads, shawls and scarves like Stevie Nicks. I wear tall shoes to off-set my smallness, and they often have floppy flowers on them.

I assured Maggie that I hadn't felt fluffy or slinky for quite a while. Sparkly, yes. I flew to California for the engagement party. We picked out the perfect outfit together: an ivory skirt with low-key red sequin (yay!) flowers and a ballet neck, open-knit cashmere sweater with sleeves. Three-quarter-length sleeves. Mom dropped me off at the airport and was there to pick me up as I took on yet another role: the "how in the world did we get *here*" moment of being the mother of the bride.

Nearly a third of American women are between forty and sixty. If we're that old, how old are our mothers? We are a big slice on the pie chart, and we, like Kerouac, with hair dryers and cosmetic cases, are on the road. My friend Patti drove from Washington State to come home to Columbus and move in with her mother. "Every place, every place," she said. "Every restaurant, every rest stop. I thought I'd make a bumper sticker: HONK IF YOU'RE WITH YOUR MOM."

"HAVE YOU ALWAYS been *this* close with your mother?" Vineyard Marcia asked one summer afternoon while she was visiting and we were sitting in the sun.

"Well, you know we've always gotten along," I told her. "But nothing like this. We're married now."

In my head, I can hear my mom saying, "Oh, Debba," afraid that this definition will somehow scare off the Fabio who is certain to be in my future. But it is what it is at the moment. Mom's my who-you-gonna-call?

Living a few nights as roommates under stiff hotel bedcovers elicits full confessions. We were visiting Bob's family in Chicago for Thanksgiving when Mom opened up to me: "Daddy and I were messy in hotel rooms."

"You were?" I couldn't believe it. My mother cannot go to sleep if her papers and her pencils are not lined up correctly. And Dad had been meticulous. Military. He used silver metal shoe trees. Never was a lid separated from its pot, never a comb not linearly lined up beside its friend the brush.

"What do you mean, you were messy?" I asked her.

"Oh, you know. We left towels on the floor and threw magazines around." I felt like I was on a rock-star road trip, such a room trasher/thrasher was my mother. Although my slovenly habits annoy her at home, she joins me in this freedom when away. It is a diplomatic art to travel well with someone. I think we've aced it.

Our conversation is an ongoing thing. It doesn't begin and it doesn't end; it is almost like talking to yourself. I'd become oblivious to how tedious this could sound to others, how irritating and exclusionary our conversations could be.

I HAD PUT my too-big house on the market before Mom and I traveled to my niece's college graduation. A window maker had built the house, so every window was different. A creek ran through the yard, and there were ducks. At first it felt like a peaceable kingdom. After four years it became Gothic, an encumbering sinkhole threatening to eat me. I was offended when an old teacher asked me, by rote, the question for single women. She had never seen my house, yet still asked it: "What, are you rattling around in there?"

No, I was not rattling around! I was happy! I was busy! I was lying naked in the sun!

Eventually, though, I started to rattle. I was on the lookout for a little house, just big enough for two papillons—my dog, Lausche, and me.

The drive from the hotel to the university was on a beautiful, tree-lined winding road with pleasant house next to more pleasant house, with fences and porches and paint jobs. Naturally, Mom and I discussed them.

"Oh, that's a cute one!"

"Oh, that's a cute one."

"Oh, look right up there. That's a cute one."

We were nattering gnats in the backseat. The rest of our family rolled their eyes and sighed and put on headphones.

When I finally tuned in to the negative effect that our continuous chat had on them, I was reminded of the time when my brother Bob and I were teenagers and our parents had gone to pick Tim up at camp. Our great-aunts invited us to eat dinner with them at a Chinese restaurant. They knew just what to order, and had recommendations for us, but the sheer excitement of being around such stimulating youngsters made them each grow a wild hair. They were both going to take the chow mein!

When the waiter brought the chow mein to the table, it was the jack-in-the-box under the silver dome. Our aunts were poised and ready. But wait, it didn't look like chow mein.

"It tastes like chow mein, but it doesn't look like chow mein," one said.

"It doesn't look like chow mein, but it tastes like chow mein," the other one said.

Variations of this went on all through dinner.

"It doesn't look at all like chow mein," said one.

"But it tastes like chow mein," said the other.

My mom and I were these aunts come back to life, talking repetitively to each other on the way to Bob's daughter Amanda's graduation. Cute houses were our chow mein. I realize now that I need to stop and remember that there are others along for the ride—that I do not own Mom just because I am the one here with her.

A few years later, Tim had moved to Florida. Mom went to be with his family for Christmas. I am possessive and do not lend her out easily. On her way home, she called from the Jacksonville airport to tell me she'd call from Atlanta to tell me she'd call from the jetway so I could be waiting at baggage when she came home.

"DON'T YOU WANT to kick the shit out of your mother sometimes?" a stylishly thin, stylishly coiffed, stylishly turned-out woman inexplicably asked at the rehearsal dinner before my daughter's wedding.

"I'm sorry?" I asked politely, thinking the din in the restaurant had distorted my hearing. You couldn't even hear the toasts.

"Don't you sometimes want to kick the shit out of your mother?" the woman enunciated. She had met my mother and heard glowing things about her. I think she was trying to be convivial, conspiratorial, even, joking ironically about Mom.

I didn't play along. "No," I said. "I never want to kick the shit out of my mother."

"What did she say?" my mother asked. She was sitting on my other side. I told her, and we laughed and laughed, and now it has become part of our lore.

Am I jealous of my mom's capabilities, her articulateness, her beauty? Do I feel bad about myself in comparison to her? Do I want to kick the shit out of my mother?

No, thank you.

I looked sufficiently mothery for Maggie's wedding procession. My tortoiseshell hair was pulled back in a hip L.A. French twist. My mother wore a silver silk pantsuit and made everyone whisper about how stunning she looked as she walked to her seat on a groomsman's arm.

My daughter, my daughter. Breathtaking always, the most elegant bride. I sat on one side of my ex-husband, John, and his wife, Cheryl, sat on the other. We all held hands.

It is a constant throughout cultures and generations that you want to live to dance at your daughter's wedding. Well, I had just seen the movie *Frida*. I began to dance as Salma Hayek did in the movie: I threw my arms in the air and clicked my fingers. I deftly draped Cheryl's pashmina around my neck and down my back and pictured a mantilla. Even during the hora, I clicked imaginary castanets.

But after the wedding, when the video came, I quit drinking. I saw myself leaping to catch the garter (first mistake) and landing on the floor in a splayed-out mess. I think both my mother and daughter—and probably that woman—wanted to kick the shit out of me.

I knew I had a problem with alcohol. The problem was I loved it. There was nothing more inviting to me than a booth and a Bud Light. I drank as a high school student, I drank as a college student. One night at a summer wedding—I think I was drinking tequila sunrises at the time—my aunt told me, "Lambie, you don't have to drink it all in one night." Booze was always big in Ohio, booze and the Buckeyes. I continued drinking in California and kicked it up a number of notches after the divorce.

I had high aspirations in newspapering, but lowly habits. Before I started my job as a columnist, I took a dive-bar driving tour of the great Southwest in a car with a hole in the floor, owned by my drinking buddy. I didn't find the Grand Canyon in any way as grand as the basement bar we discovered on the out-skirts of Flagstaff. I would be the first to suggest after-work drinks with my colleagues, and when they finally burned out on that, I discovered drinking alone. Poor Maggie. She used to beg me to drink my Gallo burgundy jug wine in fancy wineglasses. Somehow that would make things better than watch-ing me drink from the tumblers I preferred.

I was not worried about myself. I was a good-timin' gal, after all. I met a bombastic barfly to spend time with. He explained our relationship perfectly:

"She don't like to think on the weekends."

One Christmas he gave me a present bought with the cash he'd made returning the beer bottles we'd emptied. What a proud rendition of O. Henry's "Gift of the Magi." My friend Annie and I and our children were once asked to leave a Mother's Day brunch. Firmly. It was a buffet, and we thought that meant all-you-can-drink mimosas.

Back home, when Mom and I drank wine, I would sneak just a little straight from the bottle as I went to "freshen" our glasses. When we were out to dinner, she'd act as if she didn't mind when I ordered a third glass, but I saw her eyes, and she did.

I started to notice a pattern when a waiter at a

favorite restaurant called my girlfriend and me lushes as we'd meet for lunch. I'd write in my Gratitude Journal, "Got home OK." One night I threw up out the car window as I navigated my way home. The good decision to move back to Columbus was surrounded by dangerous ones, and after Maggie's wedding, that began to sink in. One night as I soaked in the bathtub, I realized I could not see clearly through drinking's double vision. To move forward would mean I'd have to give it up. That was another good decision, and one I continue to make every day.

WE RETURNED TO Florida a few times. I joined Mom for part of her book tour and rode in her jet stream. Another winter we returned to Longboat Key. Mom thought she'd try it and took a condo for a month in the resort complex she and Dad had come to for forty years. The Bob Greene T-shirt beach, the place I lay listening to their voices as Monica Lewinsky hit *The New York Times* and Dad would laugh and say, "Marvelous, marvelous," then fall asleep during the five o'clock *Simpsons*.

My mother's friends (whom she dearly loved) were here, but some, of course, had suffered loss and poor health and a lot of the couples had been halved by death. The conversations centered on this formerly active group who once walked the beach, played tennis, and drank cocktails together. Now my mother caught up on who was sick and who was sicker. Even the dogs were dying. Dolly, a beloved wirehaired terrier's, passing had saddened her family and community so much that the couple arrived with a matching Molly the next winter. It was a different place for Mom, who was raw there without Daddy. She kept saying the condo's floors were too cold and too hard, and it rained every day except one.

One night two of her friends, sisters, drove in to see us. We had shrimp on the porch, and at sundown, the bagpiper came.

We had heard about the bagpiper, that he was new this year and friendly, and sometimes at sunset he would stand on the beach and play. This was one of those nights, and we sat on the porch, one divorced woman, two widows, and a wife whose husband had Alzheimer's, listening to the words in the music the piper played. We sat straight and strong, all of us having smashed right into heartache and kept going, but tears dripped down all our faces. Amazing Grace.

We went again, *en famille*, for Mom's eighty-fifth birthday. We broke protocol and didn't write songs, but we threw in a poem or two. We returned to a wonderful resort we had gone to as children. We were, thoughtfully, in cottages within Mom's walking distance to the beach, which wasn't very far. It was a glorious, relaxed reunion. I think of my family as heliotrope. Our faces have always turned toward the sun.

For the first time in her life, the Florida sun was too hot for my mother. She sat in the shade part of the time, then went inside to lie down. We used to walk up and down these beaches; we used to scour the sand for seashells together. Now she napped in the afternoons, and I walked the beach with Tim.

I HAD A stint of traveling ahead of me. Family history went hand in hand with scrapbooking, which was surpassing baseball as America's favorite hobby. Scrapbookers wanted to learn about the journaling aspect of their projects. They wanted to become confident in the words as well as the pictures they mounted and saved on pages of meticulous design. I bought a bright red suitcase at T. J. Maxx and joined the scrapbooking circuit to help teach them how to tell family stories. Scrapbooking conventions are giant events. Lots of mothers and daughters attend together, and often a few grandmothers, too. The women stay up all night in their pajamas to work on their scrapbooks together at a "crop," this century's equivalent of the quilting bee. They take classes and go shopping during the day. I became mesmerized by the merchandise. It was a foreign, aromatic marketplace populated by women in sweatshirts with scrapbooking slogans on them. I CROP THEREFORE I

SHOP. Papers upon papers upon papers were stacked in Lucite cases, calibrated by color. Every shade of white was there, from ivory to eggshell to ice, embossed and flocked and unembossed, in florals and paisley and squares. Embossed pinkish apricot paper, sunset-colored vellum, milky tea white, amber brocade-floral print on mint-chip ice-cream green. Sensual fare.

I met a magician who was scrapbooking about her magician mother. This was in Las Vegas, which should go without saying. Her mother's mother had been a magician, too. Her book was filled with spangles, playbills, and black-and-white glossy glamour photos of three generations of magic women.

WHEN I LIVED in the ghost town, I met a Designated Daughter, oddly, through scrapbooks. Doris was in her seventies. Her mother was a hundred years old and blind. Doris was the county auditor and sat on every important board in town. I met her at a library meeting; she made an announcement afterwards. She asked if anyone might have some magazines around the house that they were finished reading, and, if so, could they bring them to next month's meeting so Doris could give them to her mother?

Few community members had many magazines at home; this was not an economically secure town. I

was still too new and too shy to ask why a blind woman
would want magazines, but I nodded and made a
meaningful face. I knew I had magazines at my house.
In fact, I could build a house of magazines. They are
big on the Maslow's hierarchy of needs in my life.
Magazines in bed, I've always told my daughter. All
you need is magazines in bed.

After the meeting, I hung around in the high
school vestibule until Doris walked out of the library. When she came through the doors carrying
three battered *Family Circle*s and a few *Ranger Rick*s, I introduced myself and mentioned that I passed her
house on my walk (climb) to the post office. I apolo-
gized in advance if mine was a rude question, but I
wondered: What did a blind woman do with magazines?

She scrapbooked, Doris said. She was famous for
it locally and had her picture in the big papers down
the mountain. Her mother cut pictures out of the
magazines and pasted the pictures in scrapbooks.
She donated the scrapbooks to the children's ward at
the hospital in the city.

"Oh, she gets such a kick out of all of this," Doris
told me.

"But can she see the magazines?" I asked.

She could see shapes. She could make out the form
of a figure. She could tear off the cover of a pretty
girl or a table setting and paste it on a page. She

enjoyed the activity, the cutting, the opium scent of rubber cement, slippery when brushed from its amber jar. She welcomed the feeling of usefulness and doing unto others. At times during the day and night, she would cry, just cry, Doris said. She was a hundred years old, blind and crying, and her seventy-something Designated Daughter was at a loss for what to do to help.

I asked whether it would be all right if I dropped some magazines on their front porch. The next day and the next day and the next, I carried two Albertsons bags full of magazines up the hill to Doris's house on my way to get the mail, where I'd no doubt pick up a new magazine or two.

At the next meeting, Doris acted as if it were manna from heaven that I'd dropped off for her mother instead of old copies of *InStyle* and *Martha Stewart Living*. Doris had squirreled away some magazines, she said, so she could dole them out in times of need. In a survivalist-minded community, squirreling away comes naturally.

I told her I would keep the magazines coming. I could not fathom my luck at having found a random act of kindness I could carry out. Random acts of kindness were all the rage in both bumper stickers and collective thought. I'd never felt that kindness was my forte, but I found it had perks. In leaving the bags on the porch, I laid down my burdens. My arms

and spirit felt so light, I thought I could fly over the
wooden sidewalks, down the hill, and home.

THE CINCINNATI AIRPORT has been a thorn in my
side more than once. I was stuck there coming home
for Thanksgiving vacation my first year at college. I
hitched a ride to Columbus with a lovely couple who
heard my plight. If memory serves, I had a turtle
with me and was wearing orange corduroy paisley
pants. More recently, I was coming off the scrapbooking circuit, tired of my own voice and anxious
to get home. All the passengers were at the gate when
we heard an announcement. There had been a security breach—someone had opened a "do not open"
door—so we'd all have to come through security
again. This meant everyone in the airport. Every
person at every gate, along with maintenance, desk
clerks, and retail salespeople.

The cooling system had been turned off as a pre-
caution, and there was a bottleneck of anxious
travelers stuffed together trying to make it down a
narrow corridor to get to who knew where, carrying
carry-on luggage.

A claustrophobe's nightmare. A germophobe's
breakdown. I was not happy, thinking about the
1979 Who concert, right there in Cincinnati, where
eleven fans were trampled to death trying to get in.
As I ground along with this group of strangers, I

spotted a tall man wearing a short-sleeved OSU golf shirt, and I decided to stick close to him. This description is not hard to come by anywhere in Ohio, but he was at the gate, going home to Columbus, and I latched on. As we were carried along by the crush of humanity, I started hatching my rent-a-car plan, which I pitched to my OSU buddy. "Pssst. Let's rent a car, split the cost, and drive the two hours home. You drive." He was good with it, particularly when we shot out of the birth canal into a sea of people waiting to take off their shoes and jackets and pass through security again.

It was then when I saw them, the old couple, an image I haven't been able to get out of my mind. He in a navy blue double-breasted blazer, she in old-age-appropriate suit, blouse, and pumps. They were dressed as they would be for a pleasure cruise, yet it was a post-9/11 sea of terror they were facing. I couldn't get near them in the crowd of stranded passengers. I wondered if they had children in town who could pick them up. I thought about Mom and how I never, ever could have gotten us down that hall.

She and I learned what we needed to about getting around airports, which changed over time and trips. At first we'd drop each other off, then, come arrival time, wait at the airport McDonald's until the other called from baggage to say we were safely home. When flying alone became a bad idea for Mom, we learned to load first after first class, of course, but lined up against the wall with the babies in the strollers. Then Mom learned how to order a wheelchair at departure, between gates, and coming home. We learned to carry cash, not only for the Skycaps but also for the wheelchair assistants and electric-cart drivers who got us from place to place. Things got physically harder for my mother. Her walking wasn't good at all.

Homeland Security was its own trip. The wheelchair person would get Mom as far as the special pacemaker gate; she'd have to totter through on her own. A female agent would put on surgical gloves and pat her down. When the agent got to Mom's bosom territory, she would explain what she was going to do and add, in a courtly way, that she would do it with the back of her hands. Did they think this way was less intrusive and would keep them out of legal hot water with sexual harassment suits of pacemaker-wearing eighty-five-year-olds? Soon traveling altogether became too physically taxing for Mom to endure—even the drive to the airport in her car was too much. After a lifetime of rides to and from, I began to park at a lot nearby and have the van man drop me off.

WHO EVER WOULD have thought a wheelchair would be a joyride?

Years ago, when we were on our way to Florida, I had caught a glimpse of a couple we knew crossing a concourse ahead of us. The wife was pushing her husband in a wheelchair, and I said to Bob, in my stupidity, "The day I need a wheelchair at the airport is the day I stop traveling." How cocksure I was, and how fast I changed. By 2002 air travel was a disaster, and I wasn't so great myself in the walking category. Tom Ridge was the director of Homeland Security, and it appeared he didn't know his ass from his elbow, as we cackling seniors like to say. Never say never. I ordered a wheelchair as I made my reservations. It's the only way to go!

When Bob and I went to Pasadena to see our first grandchild graduate from high school, the beautiful outdoor ceremony was at the school, and the reception was beyond the football field. Bob had to stop and sit down every few steps, needing to find a bench or a rock, anything. The air went out of my balloon; I was worried and saddened and angry with myself for feeling impatiently slowed down. When our grandson, Tucker, graduated ten years later, Bob was gone, and I was eighty-four. In a pouring rain, my son Tim and I went to the Steamboat Springs gym. To the top of the bleachers we went, climbing row by row. My unsure steps made me look back to when I was agile and Bob was fragile. I thought then and I am positive now that I should have just sat there for four years until our youngest grandchild, Hannah, graduates from Steamboat High.

D.G. and I embarked on a round of travels and trips, some book promotions, some family events. We were road warriors, together most of the time. We covered a lot of ground and a lot of air miles; the more miles we accumulated, the more we used. We always shared a hotel room, except once, in a high-rise Marriott near the large university from which another granddaughter would graduate. For some reason, we each had a room. We hardly knew how to communicate when we were next door instead of next bed. Without D.G. to remind me to check all the drawers, I left behind new handkerchiefs and most of my underwear. On our other trips, she was my "waitperson" in the morning, going to the lobby (in her pajamas) to bring back breakfast and bringing water to the nightstand between us at night.

The more we shared our world, the more the world around us seemed to shrink. Not necessarily of our own choosing. My contemporaries were disappearing at an alarming clip, so of necessity, I turned to Debby for companionship and sharing and going and doing. We were each running on our own track (if not running, then moving at a slow jog), and these parallel tracks were converging. I was working on a new book idea; she was working on an online project. No one had to tell us to "get a life"; we had three: hers, mine, ours.

Wherever we looked, in the malls and coffee shops and check-ins, in the lobbies and the ladies' rooms, in Tampa and Hayden, Colorado, at LAX and Midway, there we were: the fortysomethings with their seventysomething mothers or the sixtysomethings with their ninetysomething mothers; even the seventysomething with the hundredsomething mother did appear, but usually in a doctor's waiting room.

There is a pandemic of us, and as Debby and I nudge each other with each sighting, we exchange a bittersweet smile of recognition. We think we can tell at a glance which relationships are joyous, which are tedious. We watch, eagle-eyed, as the mother-daughter combo communicate or not, realizing that we are probably as often wrong as right in our snap judgments. Yet we know them when we see them, and we understand the dynamics of the Designated Daughter and the mother in need.

6

THE CIRCLE

M Y COUSIN MOLLY invited us all to dinner to celebrate her new round dining room table. Molly lives larger than most of us. She is such an impish spirit, though, we don't hold it against her. When I say "we" I mean the royal "we"; our family of women knit together by needles seven generations long. Molly polished her candlesticks, and around the table sat my aunt Sue and my other cousins, Julie and Kathy. Sally and her daughter, Jill, were there, of course; we are related through grandmothers and great-grandmothers going back over a hundred years. These women make up our safety net. If there is a crack, we will not fall through it. This is not spoken among us, but we all know it is assured. Mom is the elder, the institutional memory. Jill and I each wish we could cut off our mother's head and freeze it so it would always be there to answer our questions.

During calling hours for my father at Schoedinger's, I greeted Sally, whom I had not seen in twenty years. I hadn't seen Jill in probably longer than that.

"Oh, Jill will be thrilled you're back in Columbus," Sally told me, and I wondered why. So did Jill when her mother asked if she wouldn't be thrilled to reconnect with me. Jill and I had never been connected, except by the yarn that holds our strong women together, our Columbus centrifugal force.

Jill had decided to come home from California, too. One day she had the urge to call her mother and reached her in a giddy mood. Sally was high on painkillers.

"I was just going to call you," Sally said. "I'm in the emergency room."

"I beg your pardon?" said Jill.

Sally had gone to the beauty parlor, and while going to change into her smock, she fell down a trapdoor that had been left unlocked by a workman. She fell nine feet down to a cellar, and then another woman fell right on top of her. When the squad came, Sally was understandably in a mood. The EMTs asked her how old she was, and she growled at them, "What makes you think I'm going to tell you?"

Gales of laughter sounded from above. Sally, with a shattered ankle, the other unfortunate woman, with a broken rib, and the medics looked up from their hole. In the confusion, they had forgotten that this was Halloween, and they were in a hair salon, after all. Every stylist looking down at them in the cellar was dressed as a character from *The Wizard of Oz*. Sally's ankle was badly fractured, and Jill thought she would come back for a few weeks to help out where she could.

Jill has been home for fourteen years now. During these years her fun-loving father died, and she and Sally shepherded Jill's niece, Christy, a thirty-two-year-old mother and twin, through brain cancer. They surrounded her with love while she died. Each had assigned hours at Christy's bedside. Sally took the mornings and brought doughnuts.

Sally was right. I now could not live without Jill, who is a Designated Daughter married to a Designated Son. We were talking about cigarettes the other day, how they can really stink up a car.

"Nana's cars always smelled like cigarettes, and I used to love that smell," I said.

"Cigarettes and perfume," Jill corrected. Her grandmother Bern was Nana's friend, and they all wore perfume and smoked. What I know in deepest memory, Jill does, too.

Molly's remodeled dining room had arched scenes

of Tuscany—you feel you're looking out a window—
hand-painted on the walls. She had not been able
to find a round tablecloth to her liking, so we sat at
perfect place settings laid lovingly on a bedspread
she'd bought for the cause. We were mothers and
daughters and granddaughters, with ghost grandmothers standing behind us, and ghost grandmothers behind our mothers, all relatives, all friends.
There I sat, straddling generations. Six years into
Designated Daughterhood, and I was going to be a
grandmother, too.

I WAS TEACHING a Saturday writing class at Thurber
House, where James Thurber lived as a boy. My cell
phone rang. It never rang. I was praying that the call
was good news from my Realtor about my house,
which was for sale. I had taken his suggestion and
painted the house taupe in a conciliatory gesture.
What was wrong with people? Couldn't they see the
beauty in the yellow and green I'd had it painted
upon moving in? People referred to it as the Easter-
egg house. I thought that made me a fine landmark
on the way to the Wal-Mart.

"Hey, I thought you couldn't take calls," yelled a
child in my class, thrusting his shoulder from its
socket at a forty-five-degree angle, his hand waving
at the end of his arm like a flag at a car lot.

I had no idea whether you could take calls. I only

weekended as a teacher. "Hello?" I said into my cell phone in the tentative manner of one not used to receiving cell phone calls.

"Hello," Maggie said. We have been long-distance to each other for much too long.

"Oh! Hello! It's my daughter!" I said, pointing the cell phone at my class. They were there to learn about family history. I felt proud to prove to them I actually had family. "Say hi," I said.

"HIIIIIIIiiiiiiiiiiiiiiiiii!!!" said the class, delighted with a mass opportunity to yell. I smiled back into the phone.

"I'm in class," I said to my daughter.

"I'll talk to you later," my daughter said.

"Everything all right?"

"I'll talk to you later," repeated my daughter.

"No, what? You can talk to me now." I walked into the hallway and shut the door behind me.

"Are you out of the class?"

"I'm out of the class."

"I took a home pregnancy test," my daughter said, "and it had a faint line of yes."

I CALLED HER the second I got home.

"So," she said.

"So," I said.

"So, how do you feel, going to be a grandmother?" my daughter asked.

"Well, I have time. I have time to adjust," I answered after a moment's thought.

"Adjust?" she asked. It would be she who would be doing the adjusting, would it not?

"I'm going to go through a metamorphosis, too."

"Oh, leave it to you."

"Leave it to me what? Making it all about me?"

"That's it," my daughter said.

I KNEW THE second I was pregnant with Maggie. I knew it when I got out of bed that Sunday in August 1974. My husband had convinced me there were better ways to spend the day than going to a colleague's picnic. I believe the same intuition hit me in Target one afternoon before Maggie's call. I bought the cutest khaki blazer with pink piping inside, which I saw in the Isaac Mizrahi section. Kind of flared, kind of kicky, kicky khaki. It didn't look as cute *on*, though, when I got it home. I checked to see that it was a size small, and that was when I took time to read the label: LIZ LANGE MATERNITY.

I DIDN'T KNOW who I was. What is the combination of a Designated Daughter, a long-distance mother, and a newborn grandmother called? And who was I in the mix? I was torn. Where should I be? What

should I be doing? If mine was the sandwich generation, I felt like a six-foot sub. I felt stretched, divided, and tied down. Whatever happened to that
independent free spirit in the ghost town? I thought
about Molly's table and the connected spirits there. I
thought about how a woman with a mother must
someday become a woman without.

"YOU CAN'T TELL anybody."
  "I can't tell Wede?"
  "Well, Wede," my daughter said.

TWENTY-SIX YEARS AGO, Maggie, Wede, and I flew
to California. My then-husband, John, was already
there on the job, and we were moving cross-country
to be with him. Wede was helping us do it. I was
drinking then, and as the plane took off, I marked
the change by ordering an in-flight Bloody Mary.
This beginning proved inauspicious for me. I don't
know if it was turbulence in the air, or turbulence in
my soul, but fifteen minutes into the trip, I spilled
the drink right onto my lap. I was wearing jeans, and
the thick denim only partially soaked up the tomato
juice and booze, leaving flecks of celery salt and pun-
gent darkened liquid directly on my crotch. I made
my way to the restroom and attempted to remedy the
situation with water and paper towels, which made it

worse. I looked like I was hemorrhaging, and that was how I arrived in L.A.

I'D BE GOING back there to visit, a grandmother now myself.

I changed my hair from tricolor to some sort of clownish red, to mark the change.

I didn't recognize myself when I looked in the mirror. I saw the comedian Carrot Top with Grandma Ethel's face. Cindy at Studio Fringe has been keeping me in tricolored hair for years now. It was showstopping at first; waitresses would hurry across their restaurant floors to tell me how hip and groovy I was. My hair provided the perfect small talk in social situations.

"Oh, your hair is different again," people would say, and I'd nod, oh yes, pawing shyly at the floor with my hooves. A boy at Molly's son's bar mitzvah called me Cruella De Vil.

So I went red—very red—and when I told Mom, she went silent. My hair has been our only bone of contention; in fact, it was a bone of contention for my dad and for Nana, too. From her deathbed, Nana told me that my hair looked "a little smarmy." Dad told me my hair looked like a "fright wig."

I talked to Mom about coming over there for dinner. I was not looking forward to watching her face.

"It's bright. It's a change," I said. I was trying to both sell her and warn her.

"Well, I can like it, or I can not like it. It's your hair, and it really doesn't matter. It's you, and I love you and everything you are and the woman you've become."

"Say that when you see it," I said.

Her face tried to fake it, but I can read her mind.

On the first nice-weather day, I stopped at Mom's to help her put the white flowery cushions out on her deck furniture for yet another summer. I wasn't in the mood to hang around. I wanted to get home to *Oprah*, but Mom wanted me to stay. So, why not, I stayed and stuck my face into the sun. She said my hair looked a little brighter—maybe next time Cindy could tone it down. I told her it would fade, and we sat and we talked about times with Daddy and times with us kids and the time she told Nana I'd be moving to California.

"I was excited for you. I thought it would be like our time in the army," Mom said. "You wouldn't be weighed down with all the obligations."

"Hello, I'm back," I told her, not very nicely.

I don't like to admit that Designated Daughter-hood is sometimes an obligation, sometimes a drag, sometimes a chore. Some days I just want to be left alone, and then I panic with the knowledge that some-day that's exactly what will happen.

"WE SAW THE heartbeat," my daughter said.

"You did! Oh my God! You did?"

"We did."

"I thought you couldn't see it until your next appointment?"

"Well, we saw it."

"What did it sound like? Was it going really fast?"

"We saw it, Mom, not heard it."

"What did it look like?"

"Like a dot flashing. And it's thirteen millimeters long. And it has a tail. I think I'm having a dog."

I spent two days trying to download the ultrasound picture showing the heartbeat. My computer desktop looked like a backyard after a five-year-old's birthday party, littered with StuffIt this and StuffIt that and MIMES and JPEGs/MIMEs and aliases of the MIMES and JPEGs and finally, I dragged something into somewhere and there that baby was. The ultrasound was dark and grainy but helpfully labeled "head," "heart," and "yolk sac," with a line pointing to each part. I would swear I saw eyes in the head. This baby looked like Jiminy Cricket without the top hat.

MY BONES WERE crumbling as the baby's were forming. My doctor's office called to let me know that the bone density test showed some osteoporosis. I saw my PT Cruiser as the physical manifestation of this hereditary malady: a shrunken car next to my old SUV. As we get older, we get smaller. And don't tell me to give up my coffee. On some days—and I don't like to admit this—it feels like the only warm thing I can hold on to.

MOST OF MY friends are artists, and many have lost their mothers.

"There's before and there's after," my friend Lindsey said to me, speaking about the unspeakable after her mother died. Lindsey is building an altar, covering her entire bathroom in ceramic art, broken china, and the womanly blue Estée Lauder Youth Dew bottles her mother collected. Sparkling words spell out "I Miss Her" on the sink. My friends see how I am with my mother and feel a certain fear for me. They know what I am up against. They don't know if I can take it. Neither do I. Neither does my mother. She worries more for me than she does for herself.

Lucinda put on a group show about mothers and daughters. Each daughter was to encapsulate her mother's personality in the guise of a chair. Kathleen's mom nursed British soldiers in World War II. Her hat hung off the chair back in a flirty salute. Lucinda's mother was an artist, too, and her chair wore a smock—the real smock she wore as a graphic artist in Manhattan in advertising's heyday. It still had splashes of paints and colored inks on it. The rest of the chair was decoupaged with her mother's advertising artwork: the Audrey Hepburn—waisted women in picture hats and veils, the brides, lacy as lambs.

Jill's chair was great. There was Sally, an ashtray filled with cigarette stubs, stylish magazines, and the latest glitzy novels strewn beside the feet of the chair, which were wearing tennis shoes with glitter. Off the back of the chair, her red glasses dangled from their beaded, befuddled-professor glasses chain. Jill's mom is one in a million. We all are, the exhibit proclaimed.

WHEN LOIS'S HUSBAND, Harry, died, their three sons spoke both lyrically and hilariously. Lois made tapes for all of us labeled YOU DON'T JUST BURY HARRY. Now Lois was sick. Lois was dying. Lois had the "dimensions," as a neighbor from Virginia City used to say. Mom called me when she walked in the door from seeing Lois. Lois thinks she's at the beach, but she's in an assisted-living facility. She thought her caregiver was stealing her space, and worse, she thought she was stealing her thoughts. I was doing laundry, writing, and waiting for Marcia, who had returned from the Vineyard, to come over in the rain. I knew that any minute, the ticking consistency of Lois throughout our lives would come to a stop. Lois was falling in and out of consciousness, couldn't swallow, and her hands were mottled, supposedly a sign of imminent death. Mom went back to say goodbye, but she cried out when you touched her, Mom said. Lois had been looking for Mom in her pillowcase. Mom was with her friend when she died.

I expected Dan Rather to say, "And today in Columbus, Ohio, at three-forty P.M., Lois Hofheimer passed away." I drove to Mom's on autopilot. She had parked all the way over in the garage so I could fit in, even though I hadn't told her I was coming.

"I don't know what's wrong with me. I'm just so happy for Lois," Mom said. "This is what she's been wanting and wanting." Mom's house quickly became Lois Central, a clearinghouse of information and community outreach. It all came right through my mother's phone line to where she sat, steady as she goes, in her chair.

"What's wrong with me?" she said, her heart aching with loss, yet full of relief and gratitude for the end of her lifelong friend's indignities forced on her by the thief of thought.

I THOUGHT ABOUT my obituary. I wondered about what it would say if my dog, Lausche, wrote it: RED-HEADED GRANDMOTHER DROVE A PT CRUISER. I didn't want to end up as a spunky caricature for an "It's *My*

Retirement" advertising campaign. I dyed my hair dark again soon, with a blue forelock.

THE NOVEMBER DAY when Zachary was born, the whole family sat by separate phones, in different time zones. Maggie had a Cesarean scheduled because the baby—we knew he was a boy—was in breech position, or "arse over teakettle," as his British grandmother, Vilia, put it. I could have walked from Ohio to California in the time it was taking to get the call. We knew Maggie was scheduled for an early delivery, so what was wrong? Mag's father, John, and his wife, Cheryl, and I called each other constantly—"What's going on? Have you heard anything?" I called my mom to say "nothing yet," then we jumped off the phone like June bugs, as if call waiting had never been invented. Our family formed a coast-to-coast waiting room of nervous wrecks.

Then the phone rang. Zachary was here to add another beautiful link in our chain. Jon said, "We love you, and now you have somebody else who loves you." I called Mom and then John and Cheryl, who were just ready to call me. We laughed about who heard what first, suddenly competitive investigative reporters instead of nascent grandparents. And then I dropped to my knees, thanking God for our own blessed miracle. So I guess you could say I called God third, but I had been talking to Him all along.

MOM SAID, "I told Daddy." And then I began to cry.

I FINALLY FLEW out to California when Zachary was five weeks old. Other grandmothers in my neighborhood thought the delay was scandalous. What they didn't understand was that I'd have been more hindrance than help, more problem than solution. Mag and I have differing styles. She is more like Mom, organized and speedy, while I lean toward the loosey-goosey. She watches and shakes her head as I put away the dishes in the wrong cupboards and get caught in my seat belt every time. Suddenly, she's going to hand me their baby? They had a doula on board, a concept that I'd never heard of but commend. Jon's parents lived close by, John and Cheryl were coming down from San Francisco, and then it would be time for a visit from Fumbles.

I got in at night. The cabdriver had trouble finding their home, and of course, I had no directions for him. After a few aggravating calls to Maggie and Jon, I arrived at their door. They stood there looking so tired that they resembled a *New Yorker* cartoon about tired new parents. Zach was asleep, and we were not allowed to wake him. The three of us tiptoed into the bedroom to take the quietest of looks. He was swaddled, which, like the doula, was another new one on me.

I steeled myself to quiet my emotions and looked down into the co-sleeper and felt the physical jolt you get when you see a movie star in person. There he was—the guy I had been staring at in utero in Internet photographs sent by his father—there he was in the silken baby flesh, so familiar and glowing. Hey, Zachary, haven't we met someplace before?

It did not take an instant, not even the time it took his image to reach my retina, for me to know I was looking at my very own family, miraculously grown, and precisely the right swaddled baby whom I would get to love for the rest of my life.

LET ME TELL you about the grandmothers and the great-grandmothers and even the great-greats of all of us sitting around Molly's table. It is like an archaeological dig; this is the way I see the generations of our families. In layers. Those old German immigrants from Mittlesinn were settled in Columbus, Ohio, by the 1880s, and Henry Harmon was a successful grocer with nine children. The Harmons lived across Rich Street from the Gumbles. By 1880 two Harmons had married two Gumbles, and a Gumble a Gundersheimer, and you can begin to see why we are all here. It is obvious in an

1884 article about the Jewish residents in the capital city: "A friend from Columbus, Ohio, assures us that one half of the city's young people are engaged to the other half."

It is a lucky bunch of people in this restless world when families like ours can sit around tracing the roots back to where the roots began to intertwine.

There should have been one more chair. For Lois. She was related to each of us through every family connection. She had both Levy blood and Gumble blood. She was born three months earlier than I, so once I was born, she was in my life. Off we went to nursery school and grade school, and we were members of the same Columbus School for Girls graduating class of 1937; we will be celebrating our seventieth reunion this year. She will not be there. Lois, my lifelong friend, died of Alzheimer's disease, but she remembered me to the end.

Later, there was a sociable circle, too: the Saturday-Night Crowd. We seven couples had survived the war and came together naturally. We were high on life and looking forward to a bright future. That is what "they" promised us: a bright future. We were the great-grandchildren of those cousin-marrying cousins, now with wives and husbands from all around the country. So fourteen little Indians lived good little lives until they began to disappear one by one: first Leonard, then Ruthie, Evie, Dottie, Frannie, and Artie. I can only ask Jackie if I have the order right. She and I are all who is left.

What would my parents think of me as the matriarch? I was my daddy's little girl, and he was fifty-two when he left me. I look at his picture every day on my dresser. My brother Al looks just like him. So does our son Tim, I think. My dad sent me off to college with a letter to read on the train; he said he knew I would use my own good sense in the years ahead and that he loved me. I saved that letter, written in his distinctive purple ink, and gave it to Maggie when she went off to college. I knew she had always had her own good sense, once she got over her freshman freedom (her eyebrow ring and the boyfriend with the nose ring). Now she's a young mother with a perfect-fit husband and my wonderful great-grandchild, Zach. Good sense of the first order.

My mother, Maggie's great-grandmother, was the matriarch for so long. When she came to pick us up, she started honking a block away to be sure we were at the door, waiting. I think if I ever go to a shrink (which I don't think I should start at eighty-seven), it would be because my mother was so obsessed with being on time. She was generous to all of us, philanthropic, liberal politically, and personally tolerant, to a degree. She had standards, and we all tried to meet them. If—well, when—we failed, she did understand.

She was truly a memorable woman. She served on national boards, on the Columbus chapter of the American Red Cross, having broken through the glass ceiling, and lived a full life after losing two husbands. I never heard her complain about her loneliness. I think now that I should have spent more time with her, although she considered me a perfect daughter. Bob got tired of her saying, "I don't know what I would do without Phyllis."

I remember one of our outings with particular poignancy. We had driven to a McDonald's on Broad Street; spring had just arrived, and we decided to eat our burgers and fries in the car. She turned to me and said, so simply, "Phyl, this is nice." Not a four-star meal in Paris; not a seven-course dinner in India; just a McDonald's with a view of the state liquor store across the street and the buses going by. When you are in your eighties, "nice" takes on a whole new significance.

She ran an efficient house; the meals were good, and we learned our manners. A distant cousin I ran into at a Florida cocktail party said to me that I had a difficult mother and a difficult husband and I didn't even know it. He was so out of line, dissing my mother and my husband and me all in one sentence, that I just sputtered off into the crowd. There were so many things I could have said; if he is one of the five people I meet in heaven, I may yet have my say. Does this delayed response prove that I am not much of a matriarch? My mother would have known what to say. But my role for now suits me well. I count my sheep before I go to sleep, the sheep that belong in my flock; I have my own children, and Lois and Harry's children, and Chuck and Frannie's children. They protect me, they look out for me; they, along with that dear group sitting around the table, are my safety net. I count my sheep as I count my blessings, and as I drift off, I almost can feel the future and am comforted.

7

DOWNHILL

COLUMBUS IS TOXICALLY gray. Even the guy at the PT Cruiser dealership told me in Midwesternese that he was on "antide-pressernts" because the gray days of winter were looming. My lease was up. I was getting a new one. Cool Vanilla. We made small talk about my sunlight box while we waited on the numbers guy. My sunlight box is supposed to keep me from Seasonal Affective Disorder: S.A.D. Saaaaaaaaaaaaaaaaaaaaad is the way I pronounce it in my head. You would think they'd come up with a dye—global-warming-friendly—to shoot up into the atmosphere and turn this gray to a bearable blue. It bends us over with its heaviness and makes us walk looking down. The first year I was back in Columbus, I was pummeled and paralyzed by the days and days of grays.

Julie brought aromatherapy and whichever Bach Flower Remedy I required. Mom didn't trust aromatherapy. She thought it was the work of the devil. She wouldn't let a drop of Rescue Remedy cross her lips to mix with the medications that kept her heart beating. Finally, Jill took me to a chiropractor, a believer in the flower remedies and bird-watching. She explained my malaise to me simply: "It's March in Columbus. Who wouldn't be depressed?"

I've always said if you want to watch the seasons change, you should live near a Hallmark. But they do it even at CVS. Check it out right after back-to-school season. The orange bags and packages of Halloween candy glow from their own aisle. It is unnerving, like nature turned up in volume and hue. Nature abhors a vacuum. When the sugar-rush season of bright orange is over, the earth tones of turkeys and cornucopias ground us. We ready ourselves because we know what's coming. I watched the seasons change at my Kroger one day. A woman wheeled around three chrysanthemum plants and looked at white plastic closet accessories in an attempt, I imagined, to give herself an autumn lift. The clouds blow in and the clouds blow away.

OVER THE SUMMER I'd moved into the perfect 1950s house, with an old-time raggedy backyard I immediately fenced for Lausche. My home has the ambience of the Celestial Seasons Sleepytime tea bear cottage. At first I was loath to look at it: The website showed a gray house with scarlet shutters, Ohio State Buckeye colors, and that seemed a little much to me. In the spring, when the Realtor brought me to the house, my opinion changed. I called Mom to come take a look. She was just a few streets over at book club. When she pulled up to the address, she said, "Oh, I remember this house very well. This is Mamaw's house." The circle made manifest. Mamaw was Sue Harmon's mother, Sug. Everyone I knew as a child had been in my living room, including me. My cousins can smell Mamaw in the cupboard. I thought Zach should call me Mamaw because I lived in Mamaw's house, but he chose to call me Memaw, and I've made the place my own.

WE ARE CHRISTMAS-LOVING Jews and huge advocates of clever cards. In the beginning, when we were children and Dad ruled the cards, they were always a play on our last name, Greene. One year there was "Seasons Greeneings"; then there was "What's Behind the Greene Door"; one year we did something about Greene stamps; and once we all posed laughing, ho ho ho, because we were Jolly Greene Giants.

Mom's 2004 Christmas card was a picture of her sitting on a bearded, hatted, hard-to-see Santa Claus's red velvet lap. He was the CVS Santa. She told me that the line to get a photograph taken had consisted

of four little kids and her. The message, alongside the picture of her laughing on Santa's lap, read "Eighty-five Years and Still Together." Many recipients of her Christmas card were sure the Santa she was sitting on was me.

THERE USED TO be an air door at the F&R Lazarus department store downtown, when Columbus was still Columbus. Charles Lazarus and his wife, Frannie, had seen such a device on a trip to France. They brought the concept back to the store, and it was 1960s magic. A comfortable air curtain blew across the entrance so you could walk into the store through an invisible door. Inside, outside, inside, outside. There was no barrier. Two thousand four would be the year I saw Mom step through the air door, going from someone who took care of me to someone I would need to take care of.

It seems as if it happens in an instant, but it takes a lifetime. Our mothers go from aging to old. We Designated Daughters become familiar with crisis mode, as our mothers' well-being differs from day to day. They put their trust in us though we do not always trust ourselves. The road ahead is not going to be easy, each step a different test.

WE THOUGHT WE'D celebrate Christmas Eve at my house, and then I'd drive over to Mom's on Christmas

morning. We had to laugh at ourselves over these
past years: I'd take one picture of her, she'd take one
picture of me; solitary women without a tree.

We'd had festive Stouffer's chicken penne pesto
for Christmas Eve dinner. I remember thinking I
was a good housewife, having two in my freezer, not
just one. Food is not my thing: Whatever the op-
posite of savant is, I'm that when it comes to the
kitchen. So is Mom, who thought the Stouffer's made
a scrumptious holiday meal. The only recipe she ever
passed on to me was for something called Stay-a-Bed
Beef Stew.

We ate early, of course, maybe earlier than usual.
There had been threats of bad weather, so Mom
scurried home. The electricity went out in the
middle of the night. An ice storm hit us and hit
us hard. Things wouldn't be back to normal for
weeks.

My uncle had been wise enough to make reservations at a motel near the airport. Kathy, her husband,
Larry, and their four-wheel-drive vehicle were on
their way to pick up Mom at three A.M. There was
room for me at the inn. Did I want Kathy and Larry
to come get me, too?

I turned down the offer, being a survivalist from
the mountaintop. I wore three pairs of socks, a sweat-
shirt, sweatpants, and flannel pajamas under my

robe and put every blanket in the house on my bed, even a quilt off the wall. I may have worn a ski cap, too. I bundled in with Lausche.

Christmas morning, Christmas miracle. I had heat and power. Al brought Mom from the motel to my house. That was when I saw it happen. I took a picture of her and knew at that moment that a line had been crossed. My mother was physically under my care. This time I got to be the one to shelter and support.

In the photograph, she is sitting in my green-upholstered rocking chair, the chair I got when Maggie was a baby. This has been "my" chair in every house. Mom is sitting in it as the sun comes through the window; the ice storm of the night before is over. At least that's what we think at the time. We are cozy together in the eye of the storm. She is wearing her own light blue robe and my green socks with yellow toes and heels. Usually, she wears ladylike house slippers that resemble shoes.

The sun is hitting her as she smiles at me from behind the metro section. A few wrapped presents sit at her feet, but we are enjoying an entirely different Christmas morning. A move-at-your-own-pace, coffee-first-and-then-the-paper Christmas. Neither of us had any expectations, but I got a Christmas surprise: the belief that I could protect my mother.

Naturally, when we were settled into snug and smug, the power went out again. Mom and I decided we were motel-bound. We'd sneak Lausche in. We thought it was a hilarious caper.

We packed our belongings, including Lausche, disguised as a baby in a blanket. We drove into the motel parking lot, which was frozen and eerie. I dropped Mom off, 007-like, parked the car, and slid toward the building, and that was when I saw my first penis in a very long time. A guy was peeing in the parking lot, and I caught the sight by the light of the moon. I was excited to report this to Mom, as she, Lausche, and I made it down the smelly corridor. We did hear some fornication on our way to the room. This place was Dante's Inferno with dirty sheets. But we had our we-don't-care attitudes firmly in place, and we settled down for a fine winter's nap.

I DECIDED NEW Year's Day was National Pajama Day, and no heavy lifting was allowed. My mother was up and dressed when I called. She was making lists and putting ducks in rows. She wanted to be ready, she said, for what was to come. What came next were Days of Grace, as Daddy used to call them: days when the weather was warm and you didn't expect it to be. Days that extend sweet spring or summer. Days we got to travel and do things we used to do. Whenever Mom says "Days of Grace," she always says, "As Daddy used to say."

MY FIFTY-FIFTH BIRTHDAY arrived. Mom asked me what I wanted, and I said a cataract operation. That was what she gave me, with a note in a card she'd signed "Your Private Eye."

Birthday morning.

"Good morning," she said. "Happy birthday, darling."

"I know what I want for my sixtieth," I told her.

"What?"

"A knee replacement."

THEN THE COUGHING began. She coughed so hard at Sue and Al's one night that she felt an electric jolt in her head. I followed her home, and she took to her bed, which she never does. She didn't feel well at all. She got the flu, and she got it bad. I did what I could, which, at that point, I felt, was nothing, so we got in touch with caregivers from the past.

There is a circle of caregivers that surround our community; someone will take care of someone else until he or she dies, then move on to the next sick person. There's always the next sick person. Some will help with the meals or just "be there" in the house. Becky had helped in Mom's house for thirty years, but she was a Designated Daughter and had no extra hours to give. We knew people who had helped during Dad's sickness, during Jill's dad's sickness, during Lois's sickness. Each helping family we knew had what seemed like a thousand branches. If Felica couldn't help, Desiree could. If Desiree wasn't available, Beverly might be. We were fortunate to have people we trusted to call on when just being the daughter was not enough.

IF MOM WERE going to be spending time in bed, she'd need nightgowns. She wanted long-sleeved nightgowns, waltz-length. Maybe two. Jill and I set off to find them. We thought she'd be easier to please than she was.

She had gotten smaller, and she was small to begin with. She had gotten visibly less hardy.

Jill and I went nightgown shopping again and came up with a bed jacket.

"Are you worried?" Jill asked me, sliding nightgowns down the rack.

"Who, me? About her?"

We fell quiet and continued to look.

Jill was the moving force in my move out of one house and into the other—she packed and put boxes together and forced me to do the same. She also has a beautiful eye. When you compliment her on this, she says, "Retail." Her people are retail. They all have an eye.

Mom actually called Jill to light a fire under me to unpack my boxes when I moved to this house almost three years ago.

"Boxes aren't Debby's thing," she said, as if boxes were anybody's thing. Mom so loved what Jill did for me that she asked her to zhoosh her living room. We stole the word "zhoosh" from Carson Kressley on *Queer Eye for the Straight Guy*. It means to style, to shoot your sleeves, to spruce up. Jill and I shopped for a yellow throw (Mom hated it) and colorful pillows (Mom hated) and put tchotchkes Mom no longer cared about in a box.

We took down pictures and changed them around and had pillows made from a beautiful Chinese fabric that Jill, with her eye, had found.

Mom sat on the couch in her bed jacket at times, and then one day she was better. She decided she'd been in bed long enough, and she was going out to dinner.

"Not if you're sick," I told her.

"I'm not sick. Don't make me feel worse," she said. "You're not the boss of me."

The day after she went out to dinner, she fell backward on the living room floor. She had walked in to admire the zhooshing. She said she felt her head bounce. We went to the orthopod she'd managed to reach before she'd even called me. She was in so much pain she was vomiting. She had fractured her spine, and there was nothing to do about it except more bed rest.

"Put me on your daily visitor list," she told me in no uncertain terms.

This would not be *Tuesdays with Morrie*. This would be Mondays, Tuesdays, Wednesdays, Thursdays, Fridays, Saturdays, and Sundays with Phyllis.

———

WE LOOKED AT the good, the bad, and the ugly all in 2004. D.G. and I were still walking along—slowly, carefully— and were not thinking of the elephant lumbering far behind us. If he would mind his business, we would mind ours.

The ugly, actually, came first. It was the ice storm that made the national news and rousted me from my bed at three in the morning. On the advice of a wise someone in my online book group, I had bought a light that came on as soon as your electricity went off. It scared me out of my wits, and as I pondered what my next move should be, Kathy and Larry rescued me. Eventually, Al deposited me at Debby's heated heaven. The saga is long, but finally, I got home, and to only one burst pipe. I offered shelter to my friend, Betty, who was in worse shape than I; her heat was still off, and her roof was leaking. We had a three-day visit, and when she went home, the New Year was here.

Facing the ugly in good spirits and with family I love had reminded me once again that I could creep up on age eighty-five and surprise it. Spring was a series of graduations, and summer, my favorite season, had not disappointed me. I welcomed the heat and the humidity under the large Ohio oak trees, the breeze blowing lightly through their big leaves. The laziness of the days was a carryover from school years. Some carryover: sixty-three years. And we all made it to Florida for my eighty-fifth birthday, to the familiar sand and dunes of Longboat Key. Each year when we left, I would walk down to the Gulf of Mexico one last time to imprint that view in my mind forever, in case I never saw it again. And here I was.

Come late fall, however, I had spent some time (well, over a month) in bed with the flu and had been coughing a lot. But I was better and had gone to the florist to get some fresh green plants for the living room. After that, I went out to dinner for the first time in a long time and had a lovely evening. The next day the new little ivy plant needed watering, so, with the small watering can, I stood in my sunny, sunny living room. The February sun, blinding in the bright blue sky, came pouring in my big south-facing windows. The elephant, out of the blue (now I know where that old phrase comes from), moved up behind me and put his trunk around me and pushed me down. Flat on my back with no warning. I could hear the BOING from my head as I bounced on the carpet. It was like a cartoon character: Tom chases Jerry off a cliff, and BOING BOIIING. I thought to myself as I was lying there: This is life-changing. I moved my legs and arms. Good. This is not fatal, but it is disastrous. Yes, this is life-changing. This is disastrous. This is BAD.

So here I was, in bed again, pretty dependent: I found a notation in my calendar: "Debby, 7:00 A.M." I think that was the night I worried about what our internist, Dr. Shell, had described as a "potentially dangerous" sodium-level read.

I thought about the friendly checkout woman at Kroger who was a cancer survivor, and the clerk at the cleaners who had written a book about her daughter's pony, which she wanted to get published, and Gary the pharmacist, who was moving to another CVS. Did they realize they hadn't seen me for weeks? When would I get back to my real life?

8

UPHILL

OM'S LIFE WAS now in the clown-punching stage: the balloon clown with sand in the bottom, built to bounce right back, punch after punch, and that was exactly what she did. In early November things had improved enough that Felica watched out for Mom while I went out to see Zachary and his parents, of course. I had forgotten that babies live in a musical world, from wind-up mobiles and lullabies to CDs. Zachary had music all the time, and for these few days away, I let it permeate me. When I said goodbye at the airport, I had his music in my head. "Trot, old Joe, trot, old Joe, you trot better than any horsey I know" and "Dinosaur, dinosaur, lonely and blue" (he finds a friend in the end, don't worry) and my optimistic morning favorite: "I feel, I feel, I feel like a morning star." Zachary pronounced it "mo-neen stah."

When I got on the plane, I was sick as a dog, and when I got back to Columbus, I was sicker still. Of course I was. I always got sick on planes. I knew it and tried to prevent it, but a trip to California always knocked me out. At home, I found that my furnace (in service since 1951) had been knocked out, too. It had been making a steel-against-steel noise. A man came and said I needed a new one. I lay sick in my bed, listening to furnace men install it through the air duct on my bedroom floor.

TIMMY'S FAMILY CAME for Thanksgiving, and I was very nervous about Mom. We sat in the living room, waiting for Tim's cab to arrive. Mom's hands were freezing. What did that mean? I insisted she put on a pair of gloves. I went to the hallway closet and got the black leather ones out of her coat pocket. "If it doesn't fit, you can't acquit," I told my mother, waiting for my brother. I was anxious for him to get there; I wanted to shift some of these responsibilities onto his strong shoulders. I felt like Sisyphus trying to get Mom and me up the hill.

A side effect of Designated Daughterdom is something I call morbid mind. One thought leaps to a worse thought and then to a worse thought until you find yourself wondering if your mother will still be here at the end of this roll of Bounty paper towels or this box of coffee filters. It is deadly to spend too much time looking through morbid-colored glasses, but they are always on your bed table. If I succumb to morbid mind, who will be there for Mom?

Tim called when he got back to Florida. He wanted my take. I told him her body could just be wearing out and we'd have to face it. By Christmas Mom was so weak, she did not go to the Harmons'. This was indicative of how sick she felt—not to go to the Harmons' was to break with tradition. I went alone and thought about how awful it would be if I were going to the Harmons' alone for real.

She looked like a bookmark in her bed, so sick and small was she. "Oh, Debby," she told me when I sat on Daddy's twin bed a nightstand away from her own. "I don't want you to have a sick mother."

That's the way she thinks. That's the mother I have.

"We'll be fine and dandy," I sang, "Lord it's like a hard candy Christmas."

Another day, before the year was over, I found myself singing a dirgeish bluesy rendition of "Can you tell me how to get, how to get to Sesame Street" to Lausche in my kitchen.

WE THOUGHT WE'D found a caretaker to come in a few hours a day. Someone to make meals, to shop for groceries, to straighten Mom's bed and such. And then we thought we'd found another one. Along with the ups and the downs in health came the changing of the caregiver guard.

Then Mom's furnace went out, like mine had. She had to get a new one. She, too, did the dealings from her bed. At times she'd creep down to the middle of the hall to look at the thermostat but her back hurt so much it made her cry.

I think it is safe to say that the two dead furnaces were a symbol. Mom and I were worn and worried, trying hard to safeguard the positive energy that had kept us going. We were experiencing a power outage. We were spent. Then one morning I called her, and she sounded more relaxed and happy than I'd heard her, maybe ever. She had finally taken a Percocet. It was like talking to Timothy Leary.

"*Und?*"

"I feel Wonderful," she said. "Kind of floaty but Wonderful."

"I told you you'd love drugs," I said.

"Well, I don't know what it is, but I'm feeling Wonderful," she said.

After a day or two, though, the Percocet went into the hall closet with the extra Dove soap and tissues. It was "binding," and my mother feared constipation more than the pain of a broken back.

She weighed 108 one morning. Her usual weight

is 124. I am gaining what she's losing. I look in my mirror and see a mixture of Roman Polanski and Keith Richards. I notice all the dead Christmas trees out in the neighborhoods as I drive back and forth from her house to mine.

MOM'S LEASE WAS up on her Chrysler (which still had the new-car smell three years later), so she bought a new one over the phone from her bed. She got someone from the dealership to come over and do the yards of paperwork, pick up the old car, drop off the new car, and likely change the keys on her key ring for her. Her key ring is rectangular clear Lucite (from the 1970s Lucite-gift era) and it says PHG in blue. Holding her keys is like holding her hand. I drove her new car more than she did.

ALONG WITH HER back, her heart was failing. Her sodium was either up or down, her potassium somewhere in between; then there were vitamin K and Coumadin levels and ProTime checks and pacer checks. Mom has weak and leaky valves with atrial fibrillation thrown into the mix. Her body is a tiny test tube. You've heard about a butterfly flapping its wings on the other side of the universe creating a tidal wave somewhere else? One lettuce leaf can send Mom's body chemistry reeling. She knows exactly how many crawls it takes to reach the middle of her bed. Five crawls. She sleeps in a twin.

Cornie, Dr. Shell's nurse and our kind advocate, called. Mom thought she sounded concerned about the results of an echocardiogram. Reading her tone, Mom assumed this meant she had about three weeks to live. Mom wanted the cold, hard truth from Dr. Shell. He told her the numbers weren't that bad. Mom leaped through the burning hoop of fear without me.

"I'm so glad I didn't call you," she said when she finally called me. "I kept thinking to myself, I'm going to have to tell Debby."

I question my ability to protect her, but she is always protecting me. Every hill we climb and conquer, Mom says, "Dodged another bullet," then looks skyward. I thought I found a bullet in my driveway, and as scared as I was about finding a bullet, I saw it as proof from the universe. Then it turned out to be a drill bit. She got weak, she got better, she got better, she got weak. We worked around it. We definitely had a new normal—you could tell by our discussions about dying in your sleep as a positive, and whether ninety is the new sixty.

Then her house went out from under her. If furnaces and bullets aren't symbolic enough, how about a shifting foundation?

At our family's last reunion in 1996, my father

told me that my brothers and I would be responsible for keeping up the property after he was gone. "Mother can't do it herself," he told me.

"Don't worry, Dad," I told him. "We're good kids."

Good kids. Old children. We are caring, but we're not contractors. If the job were to fall to me, it would be *Grey Gardens* for sure.

Every summer, Mom hired Quality Pool and the Yard Barbers in an attempt to keep the flower beds full and the pool crystal-clear, the grass and bushes neatly trimmed. A swimming pool needs daily attention. Mom would struggle down the hill to check the pool machinery when she couldn't even keep her balance in the hall. She felt duty-bound to keep everything up to Dad's standards. The swimming pool was their country club, a destination spot on Sundays where all their friends gathered. When I got married in the backyard, tiger lilies floated on the turquoise water.

Finally, the pool imploded. Sinkholed in on itself. My mother arranged to have it filled in and grassed over. It looked like a grave site. Erased.

"Can you mourn a place?" she asked as we looked out from the deck at the space, which truly had held the sunshine of our lives. We both knew the answer.

WE SPENT A beautiful Mother's Day in Mom's backyard. A friend had stopped by to see her. He called me to look at a place in the dirt beside the house, where the tip of a rock was sticking up out of the ground. It looked like a crystal, the kind I used to find in the mystical mountains of Virginia City. So he dug, and out came rose quartz the size of a dachshund. I took a Polaroid of it, and Mom, the nonbeliever, and I drove up to Gentle Winds the following Monday.

Gentle Winds is a spiritual store with classes about chakras and auras. Healers work there. I connect strongly with Cheryl, the sparkly girl, who shimmers from within and without, aided by the glitter on her face and in her short, short hair. The sparkly girl is an intuitive. I wanted her to meet Mom and explain the crystal's bigger meaning.

"They are thanking you," she said to my mother.

"Who are thanking me?" my mother said.

"The spirits, the goddesses in the earth. They are thanking you for taking such good care of the land," the sparkly girl said.

My mother softened. We knew how hard she had been working at it, how difficult it had been, and we thought the spirits had excellent manners.

MOM'S BACK WASN'T getting any better. She had additional X rays. Her spinal column looked like the last days of Pompeii. She was diagnosed with stenosis—

the devastating pain we knew well because that was what Dad had had. "So I have stenosis. I'll have it," she said as we walked out of a doctor's office. We actually have fun, if you can believe it, sitting in doctors' waiting rooms, quipping like the Gilmore Girls. We finally saw a pain doctor. I know I'm saying "we" when Mom is the patient, but that's who we've become. This doctor suggested reasons why Mom may have fallen in the living room in the first place. Besides drugs, there was not much hope for a flexible future, but there was a tight-fitting garment that did help some people. "It fits right here," she said, "right here under your boobies."

I saw Mom recoil in her chair as if thrust by a rifle kickback. It was imperceptible to the doctor but loud and clear to me.

Boobies? Boobies? My mother did not have boobies, my mother had a bosom. A bosom is what ladies such as she have. (I have tits.) I called her on it in the car, and she 'fessed up. The booby bit had bothered her. We don't even have to talk to communicate anymore.

Another time we were discussing my brown coat. Whether it could go for another year.

"You don't have to finish that sentence," I said.

"What do you mean?" she asked.

"The brown coat could go another year if I had it cleaned," I told her.

"How did you know I was going to say that?" she demanded.

WE WOULD GET out and about. We called our outings Pee-wee's Big Adventures. We'd go to Nordstrom for shoes, which seldom worked, and to Talbots, which would usually call for another trip to return the item. Mom was too tired to try things on in stores.

And we went to funerals. There were plenty of them. You could almost call it a social life. Funerals provide such release for me, they could be a day spa. I cry at obituaries, for God's sake. I go through the five stages of grief for every listing. I sometimes think I should attend strangers' funerals, the way others go to sad movies. A funeral is a surefire way to get my tears out.

We went to June's funeral. June was the mother Mom used to walk our neighborhood with, pushing us babies in strollers. In the pew in front of us was another neighbor, Pam, and her mother, another Phyllis. We were family related by two blocks in our storybook tree-lined suburb.

At June's funeral, the congregation sang "Amazing Grace."

"I ain't singing," I told my mom. I closed my eyes and listened to the music. By the time they got to "wretch like me," my tears fell so hard and fast they hit the pew beside me. A flash flood of tears that I could

not tend to any longer, tears that broke loose from the
pressure of being optimistic when life for Mom was
getting harder and harder. Each funeral is practice for
the one you know is coming. Every funeral is another
foot forward, and I don't feel strong enough to go.

MOM DOESN'T WANT Hebrew at her funeral, but
she promised she'd have some in there for me. Hebrew brings instant healing tears from a wailing wall
in my spine. I hold hands with Mom at each ceremony we attend now, and I listen to her heartfelt
recitation.

> Thou shalt love the Lord, thy God, with all thy
> heart, with all thy soul and with all thy might.
> And these words, which I command thee this
> day, shall be upon thy heart. Thou shalt teach
> them diligently unto thy children and shalt
> speak of them when thou sittest in thy house,
> when thou walkest by the way, when thou liest
> down and when thou risest up.

The way she says these familiar words is a pledge of
allegiance. This is the kind of thing I'm noticing
now. I see, I hear, what I'm going to miss.

THE NEWSPAPER HAD been thrown in the gravel,
which was aggravating, my mother said. It meant she

would have to walk around the stoop to get the paper. Mount Everest. She was afraid of stepping down from her front door.

"Or I could hook it," she said, "with Grandpa's cane." Grandpa's cane was in the front closet. "I think Grandpa only had it for show."

"To be natty?"

"I think so," Mom said. "Or Daddy used to have this thing he put his socks on with. Maybe I could use that. There are grippers. Sukie has one, I think," she said. "The next time I get one of those catalogs, maybe I'll order a gripper."

"You just got one of those catalogs," I said. "And you threw it away." She had, too. Adamantly and summarily.

"I did, didn't I," she said.

"You did. I told you you might need it."

"Well, I made a mistake."

"Everybody's allowed one," I said to my mother.

"You know I am itchy to get things done," she said to me.

"Well, maybe you might"—we are not allowed to say "you should"—"have to slow down a little."

"Not on your life," she said.

She's eighty-six, and it's beginning to show. I found a copy of an e-mail I wrote to an old friend at the time, summing up my life in as few words as possible: "Me, my mom, who has been so fun and healthyish, is suffering heart failure now. So that sucks."

She felt good and bad, up and down, and I felt like walking, talking responsibility. I called my brothers to tell them how worried I was because she found David Sedaris sad instead of funny.

WE SAT IN the car in the handicapped space in front of Barnes & Noble. Mom did not have the energy to make it past the Starbucks stand.

"If you had any idea how mad this makes me," she said.

"I know," I said, "I know," knowing what I do not want to know. "I know how mad this makes you. This should make you mad." Whenever she gets mad or frustrated, her mind jumps to someone who has it worse, which makes her feel as if she has no right to complain.

"Rail, rail," I reminded her.

"That's not what we were taught to do."

"So rail, already. Poof. Break the rules! If not now, when?" I pleaded, trying to catch her attention with a little Rabbi Hillel.

"Oh God," my mother said, looking at me suddenly. "I am Great-aunt Fanny Harmon, and you are me taking her out for a Sunday drive."

ONE DAY SHE called, thrilled, and asked me to guess what she'd just done.

"I backed out of the garage, drove up the driveway, and it was a lead-pipe cinch!"

"I'm so happy for you!" I told her, and I was.

"You should be. You should be happier for you."

"You mean I don't need to take you to your Thursday hair appointment anymore? Live strong, Lance," I told her.

Then another giant leap for womankind. She drove to the corner for corned beef because Bob was coming to town. She could get up and go again. She could do for herself. She didn't need anyone to do for her.

We were walking out of Nordstrom on one of our days out, me holding our purses, our coats, our shopping bags, and a cup of coffee. She assured me she was all right on her own; I have a tendency to smother. I watched her toe catch on a curbstone, and I watched her fall down in slow motion, like a horror movie when the thing you fear the most actually happens. I couldn't scream, just squeaked "No, no," as I caught a glimpse of a sturdy man running across the parking lot to help. My mother turned midfall to face me with the focused intent of a gymnast and the grace of a ballerina.

"I'm okay, I'm okay," she reassured me before her body hit the ground.

Every time I go to Nordstrom now, I see her body as a chalk outline on the asphalt.

After the fall, we sat in the car. She was fine, or acted like she was. A little shook, maybe, but not to worry, she said. I couldn't drive. I had a meltdown, quivering and crying, dropping Rescue Remedy drops under my tongue at a rate of twelve times a minute. I tried to pull myself together, to take deep breaths and exhale slowly.

Gently, my mother told me that she didn't want me to be the person with her if—no, when—something happened.

"Why?" I asked, traumatized by watching Mom fall and not being able to do anything about it. "Because you can't count on me? Because I wouldn't be responsible?"

"No, no," she said. "Because you care so much."

D.G. SAT IN my bedroom, and we rested. And rested. I was down for the count, and I felt as if the referee was just about to say, "seven." The hill ahead was steep and "hawd" to do. This was Maggie's comment the first time she sat on a real toilet seat, and it's now Debby's and my sad little attempt at humor as we try to get a handle on something that really is hard to do: make my back feel better.

I am not overly concerned with my health; I have great faith in my doctors, and I let them do my worrying. I am worrying about my house.

While I was bed-resting, my thermostat began its own rest. We have only used one cooling and heating company since Bob stopped shoveling coal around 1950, when we got a gas furnace. I called them. When they arrived, they told me they could not replace what was a very reliable thermostat—it was no longer available—but on their truck they had a proper replacement: It talked. We had a car once that talked, and it got on our nerves; a heckling Thunderbird like an angry parrot that had something to say as soon as we walked into the garage.

Should I (or the furnace experts) not have foreseen that the talking thermostat would not work because the furnace was almost terminal? I entertained the salesman from my bed and chose the furnace he recommended. The new chimney would fit inside the old chimney, and we would be warm and toasty as soon as the new furnace was in. In two freezing-cold days.

Once we had heat, I winced and crept down the hall and made my way into the kitchen to meet the installation crew and let them explain the problem they'd found. The new exhaust was too big to fit into the old chimney, or the EPA would not allow it, or they didn't know how to wing it, or for whatever reason, they were forced to run fat white PVC exhaust pipes out of the house, right beside the front door. Out and up. It looked as if I had a small submarine in the lower level.

I think that every widow finds herself with the same dilemma: "They" tell you to wait a year after your husband dies to decide whether to move or to stay. Here I am, almost eight years a widow, still struggling with the same old question. And still wondering who the knowledgeable "they" are.

The furnace pipes were rerouted another direction, and I felt better, and then my house problems really began.

I might have to move both my house and me uphill. It is right there in black and white: I am starting down the real, the actual, the grassy slippery slope.

My beautiful albeit forty-year-old house was a mess! There was a crack above the doorway from the living room to the dining room that had been there since Bob died. I decided just to "live with it."

In the summer of 2000, Tim, whose field has always been real estate, was home for the Fourth of July gathering. He mentioned that we needed to do something. Not that I did, until he announced in October that he was bringing Cynthia and her daughter here for a post-Thanksgiving weekend. Hmm, I thought. Hmm, bringing his lovely new lady friend home to meet his mom. Now I did care. I am not *Architectural Digest,* but I am a little *House Beautiful,* and I didn't want Cynthia to think that Tim's mother was nee Joad. I called the painters, who sent their best man to patch, tape, repair, and paint the wall.

About four months after the first painting, and a few months before Tim and Cynthia's wedding, the cracks reappeared. The poor receptionist at XXX Paint, Inc., got an earful from me. "How," I asked, "could you do such a superficial job? Are you sure you taped it before you spackled? Did the spackle dry before you painted?" To get the harridan (me) off the phone, they came and redid the work. Four months later, there were the old familiar cracks. Again.

I needed more than a painter; something major was happening under my very feet. It was time for the insurance company to get involved, and that involvement included an enigmatic engineer. The house slipping down the hill is not a metaphor for anything but that the house is actually physically slipping.

Thus began a round of contractors, estimates, one opinion, another opinion, until I, in analysis paralysis, had Tim make the decision for me and we began to keep me up on the hill.

In my mind, it was a three-act play. Act 1: the myriad troubles. Act 2: A neighbor, driving by, decided she wanted the house. Always loved this house. Always wanted a pool. I started house hunting in the beautiful new condos being built up and down my street. The neighbors came often to watch the work and the workmen; we had wine on the deck; they were assured of a *very* sturdy home. Tim wrote up a contract. We did not hear from them for weeks. Tim finally called them; they had trouble with the financing, so "thanks anyway." Curtain.

Act 3: When I was a little girl, there was a candy treat, a woman-shape made of wax, filled with tiny colored balls that were sweet. After you ate the candy, you could eat the wax woman herself. Thus, as I entered stage left, I appeared as a woman made of pills. The pills had started to fill me up from my feet. They were now about waist-high, and I thought I was ready to return to what passed for the real world: the Metropolitan Club, the book group, the beauty parlor, and a lot of funerals. Twice I tried physical therapy, walking on rubber mats and sitting on rubber balls. The audience stood and applauded. The audience was Debby.

My old friend, and stepbrother, Chuck, with great effort, came to visit. What a sport—wheelchair, nurse, oxygen, and he still arrived with crabmeat. His daughter, Peggy, brought lunch, and Stuart, his son, brought dinner, and then I was tired out. I went back to whiting out events on my calendar. I stopped pretending that I was in charge. I went to the Coumadin Clinic on a much too regular basis.

One day when Della was taking my blood pressure, she noticed a black-and-blue mark on my arm. Not unusual for me, but the shape of the bruise suggested someone had grabbed me. "Has anyone been hurting you or been mean to you?" Della the experienced, observant technician asked. She had been drawing my blood, and Bob's before me, for years; she surely did not think I was a candidate for elder abuse. Or is every single older person vulnerable? When we came out of the lab, D.G. was there, holding my coat and purse, asking if I was okay.

"As you can see," I told Della, laughing, "this is my abuser."

Abuse is hard for a layperson to define. The law has its own interpretations, yet I know what I am looking at when I hear a daughter chastise her mother for forgetting her copy of the doctor's orders for a blood draw or I listen as a woman in a wheelchair tries to maneuver the bathroom for a urine sample and the daughter sits unconcernedly in the waiting room. It breaks my heart to see old women alone at a lunch counter. Years ago, when I thought I would never be old, I heard about a woman, the wife of a psychiatrist, who would allow her mother to call only at a certain time of day.

After I wrote *It Must Have Been Moonglow*, I heard from widow after widow; we all were suffering in the surprisingly same way. Some of us were lucky enough to have options about what to do next. I still weep for the widow whose only choice was to go into some kind of senior housing where no pets were allowed. Her dog was her heart's designated companion. What she wanted me to know, what she wrote about, was how brave the dog was when they came to take away her pet, her love. She and the dog looked at each other and spoke with their eyes.

9

STAY-AT-HOME MOM

I AM A MOTHER as well as a daughter. I am not as good a mother as I am a daughter at this point, and I wonder if you can be both at the same time. Maggie does great in her own life and doesn't seem to need me. Mom does. But I need to be a grandmother. I hate showing outdated pictures of Zach. "Oh, he is *so* much more brilliant now," I'll say.

I flew back to California and spent a few sunny days. When I hear Zach call me Memaw in person, I die. He is my happy, laughing boy. I'd left Lausche with Jill while I was away. Maggie's husband got a call on his cell phone from Jill. I must have left his number in my extensive Lausche babysitting list. Jill asked to speak to me and calmly told me that, sorry for the indelicacy, Lausche had blood in her bowels.

I went panic and manic. I asked Jill to take Lausche to the vet immediately and to have the vet call me as soon as he could. I don't even think I said "please." Jill had it under control—Lausche wasn't used to the food at her house—and after I settled down from code blue, I started thanking God that Jill's call hadn't been about Mom.

Sitting with Maggie and her friends at Annie's daughter's wedding, I inquired after their mothers, whom I had not seen since these girls were in high school. Maggie's friend Alice's mother, Rita, was widowed the week of Alice's wedding. "She has this dog," Alice said. Another friend, Erin, said her mother, Sandy, was doing okay. And she had this little dog who was her world.

I pulled out my cell phone and showed them the picture of Lausche that I keep as a screensaver image. Empty-nest women and their dogs form supreme relationships. One can complain all she wants, while the other doesn't even have to talk.

THE NEXT TIME I visited California, Maggie and I put Zach in the stroller and did a round of Christmas shopping. Mom had mentioned that her friend Mary had the most comfortable-looking "leisure suit," so we strolled into Talbots. I looked at a teal-blue velour jogging suit. I knew it was not Mom's blue—a powder blue as clean and clear as her eyes—so

I started looking at a black one, but I didn't want to get her a black one.

"You don't want to get her a black one," Maggie said. She reads my mind like I read my mother's. "Get the blue. Blue is blue," Maggie said.

"You're right. Nothing's perfect," I agreed as the saleswoman wrapped the teal-blue suit in tissue.

As Mom's body got tinier and tinier, her essence became even larger to me, like Woody Allen's mother in *New York Stories* in which she took up the entire sky. I got off the plane back home, sick, again. I called both Mom and Maggie to say safe and sound. I could hear something extra in Mom's voice when she told me how glad she was that I was back.

"You don't do so well when I'm away," I said to Mom.

"I do okay."

"You don't do as well."

"No, I really don't do well at all," she said.

THERE COMES A crossroads on this journey where our mothers need more help than we can give them. We Designated Daughters try to let go of our illusion of control. Our boundaries shrink again as our mothers are confined to home. Mom is afraid she is turning into Nana—which, of course, she is—with her phone, her reading material, her remote, her calendar, her address book, her glasses, pills, and a bottle of water on her table within cockpit reach of her chair. With plenty of books lined up to read, safe harbor doesn't feel so confining at all. "This is exactly what I thought I'd be doing in old age," she told me from her chair in her teal-blue jogging suit.

We spent low-key time. We tested the fax part of the printer/scanner/fax that Tim sent Mom for Christmas and—surprise of surprises—we couldn't get the faxes between our houses to work.

I called her in the morning. "How are you?"

"Fine."

"Liar."

"I'm fine."

"You're lying."

"Well, white lies. I'm fine, but I feel like shit."

"Energy?" I asked her.

"Fine."

"Lie lie lie lie lie lie. This has been going on for six weeks."

"I'm just as happy to sit," she said.

HELPERS COME AND helpers go, doing the things that Mom can't do. When she bends over to put dishes in the dishwasher, her back hurts so much she screams.

And where am I? Ms. Dishwasher Raison d'Être of the early days? Driving back and forth, feeling guilty. Feeling that I'm not doing enough. Feeling that I *am* not enough.

Mom talked about hiring "a companion."

"Who could that be except me?" I asked.

"I need you to keep me laughing," she said. "That's what you're for."

IT WAS A gloomy rainy day, and Mom had thought better about going out for dinner with her friend Jackie to Giuseppe's, where you have to park and everything. She'd call and cancel, she said, and Jackie would understand. My friend Lindsey and I went out that night. The gloom got to us, too. We got home at seven-twenty.

Mom and I talked about how we felt like cell phones that had used up their minutes. We tried to look on the bright side of boring. Jan Struther said it best in *Mrs. Miniver*, even though I had to look up "subfusc."

> This dusty and tedious little patch of time—could she safely label it "drab" and have done with it, or would she find herself one day living through a period so relentlessly subfusc that this present lozenge would seem, by contrast, gay?

One day I felt so dull that the words dribbled out and formed a puddle of self-pity. We were at Bob

Evans when I said to Mom, "Why don't we just go sit at the cemetery and wait?"

"Oh, Debba," she said. My ennui is a downer to my mother.

"Pollyanna the Glad Girl," I said, slapping a smile on my face.

MOM CALLED. WOULD I do her one little favor and get down the sewing kit from her closet? The sewing kit was the only thing I really remember nagging about as a child. I saw a picture of it in the S&H Green Stamps catalog. I knew how many full books Mom had in her drawer, and I knew we could Green Stamps afford it. It was round wicker with a checkerboard pattern and a furry poodle. I wanted it badly, talked about it incessantly throughout the day, and definitely whined. It was summer. Mom got up off the porch after dinner in her Bermudas, so tired, three kids, hot day, and took me out to Miracle Mile, the world's first shopping center on Broad Street, to redeem the stamps. Now it's on the top shelf in her sitting room closet, and she can't reach it.

Her nightgown, her good nightgown, the one she used to wear only for travel, had ripped and made her look like Janet Jackson at the Super Bowl, she said.

I tried to sew it with her in it. She didn't have the energy to take it off. We talked about Kay, the seamstress who used to work behind a curtain at Jensen's cleaners, and about Madge and her sister, Sissy. Madge tailored Nana's clothes. As a child, I loved to go there with Nana. I'd play with the ribbons Madge stored in a drawer in Sissy's bedroom.

I brought the sewing box back down Broad Street and home with me. I called Jill. I am a collector of family detritus and knew the buttons inside would tell a story. Jill called Julie. We sat around my dining room table, sewing box in the middle, in a spontaneous grab of time. They decided to zhoosh the box. They separated the buttons into types. There were lots of heraldics, lots of Dad tans, and lots of Mom light blues.

"Phyllis still has this outfit," Julie said. Julie and Jill sorted jumbles into piles and subpiles. They held up the pretty ones for me to look at. They helped me think I could keep things in their proper order, stowed away safe and sound.

I NOURISH MOM the only way I feel I can, by never letting her run out of books. Meals are the responsibility of the ever-changing caregivers we've come to rely on. My mother and I both know my limitations. My brother Bob gave us both DVD players and a Netflix subscription. Mom was worn out, and her head hurt. I looked through her library downstairs to see if I could find her anything she liked before to read for a second time. She's donated many books to the Friends of the Library, and going through the ones left downstairs, all I could find were books by our family and shelf upon shelf of Dad's favorite subject, World War II.

We both find more sustenance in words than in food. She brought me library books when I was home sick from school as a child. She brought me Dodie Smith's *The 101 Dalmatians* when I was in the third grade, malingering. When it became a popular Disney movie, I wondered if someone at the Disney company had found the story that way, too, as a dreamy child staying home from school to read library books in bed.

One of the worst things Mom and I can imagine is to be stuck somewhere with nothing to read. It was going to be a long, hot summer weekend. The weather had been in the nineties and "unhealthful" for days. Mom had finished up her book club book by Friday, so I began to pull selections from my bookshelf to get her through the weekend. I dropped them at her house: *Prozac Diary*, Lauren Slater; *Drinking: A Love Story*, Caroline Knapp; *Journal of a Solitude*, May Sarton.

Nine-thirty Saturday morning.

"I found those books you left me very depressing," she said after "Good morning" and "How are you, darling" and "How did you sleep." "I think if you were depressed and you read these books, they'd depress you more."

ONE OF HER helpers began showing up late, each time with a different story.

"I've got a hunch," I said to Mom.

"Which is?" Mom said.

"Go to the closet with the Kleenexes. Isn't that where you put your extra medicine?"

"Yes," she said.

"Check the Percocet bottle."

"Oh, no," she said.

"Indulge me," I said.

She did. I heard her put on her shoe-like slippers and walk to the closet. She came back to the phone.

"Three left," she said. Mom had taken only two or three in her whole Percocet career.

"She be gone," I told my mother.

"Do you really think?" she asked.

"She be gone. This is what you hear about happening to other people. There's absolutely no question."

"I'm calling her now," Mom said, and that was that.

SALLY WAS THROWING a party. Mom thought she could go, then thought she couldn't, then thought she could, then decided she couldn't. "I don't want to sound like I'm feeling sorry for myself, but I hate to be the town invalid," she said. I got mad for her. I found myself in the angry stage of grief. "We're small people," I told Mom. "We're too small to hold this all on our shoulders." I got a vision of us as salt-and-pepper shakers sitting in the middle of an otherwise empty table. One weekend I freaked. First I called Becky to make sure she agreed with what I was thinking. Then I called my friend Ellen in tears. Did she know somebody, anybody, who could help my mother? "Well, my sister," Ellen said. I pushed the phone buttons and got Ellen's sister, who cried with me because she was taking care of someone else. But she'd try to think of someone, she said. In the year that followed, Ellen and her sister would lose both their father and their mother as well as Ellen's beloved husband.

We were in a bind. We admitted we needed help. I am a fine caretaker, Mom and I lovingly acknowledged, but only up to a point.

Then Jehovah sent Lisa. Lisa, one of Jehovah's Witnesses, had asked Jehovah for someone to care for. Jehovah sent her to Mom, but first she had to pass through me.

Having been burned by the drug-stealing helper, I was not about to let in anyone whom I had not thoroughly sized up. I had to do what Dad would have done. I would have to trust my own judgment. Thank God my drinking was behind me. I mentally transformed myself before our meeting. I puffed my chest out, like a man, and drew my five-foot-three-quarter-inch self up into a big badass. I pulled my car into Mom's garage and strode down the back hallway in my heavy biker boots, and then I reached the kitchen. There stood this calm and competent, lovely feminine presence. Her smile spoke of truth and good intent.

But still. My job was to take care of Mom. Though I was not loosening my grip, I could no longer do it alone. I had to share. And I had to choose the right person. I had to trust Lisa, which meant I had to trust myself. We stood talking. I took a quick history as I looked right into Lisa's eyes. They told me the same thing her words did.

I told Lisa she would never meet anyone like my mother, and I drove away feeling that now we'd make it. I added "Turn it ovah to Jehovah" to the revival meeting of affirmations that I keep at the ready in my head. Lisa moved into my mother's lower level. The burden I'd been denying was lifted. I did not have to continue carrying all the worry alone. I did not have to be any stronger than I was. I was fine as is. I was free to be sad and let loose the tears I saved for other people's funerals. And, I knew the day that

Mom needed a live-in caretaker, another milestone had been passed.

SUNDAY-NIGHT *SOPRANOS* AND one of the last of the *West Wing* episodes and should we go to Outback and it is so tiring for her to get dressed. This was our nine-thirty A.M. conversation. I should be at Mom's by five-thirty. When I got there, she was watching golf, like Nana, but really didn't care about the outcome because Tiger Woods had gone home. We pulled ourselves up out of our Sunday-evening laziness and decided what the hell. We drove carefully out of the garage and down the block, then took a daredevil U-turn into the Outback parking lot. It was too loud in the restaurant, and too cold, and Mom had to climb up a step into the tall booth. The waiter checked in with us in a staccato of niceness, even though we knew what we would "take" before we got there.

Mom and I discussed *Crash,* since we both had watched it on Netflix. We discussed how Daddy already would have asked the waiter to tell the manager to turn down the music.

I looked at her, tapped out.

"*Und* nothing," I said.

"*Und* nothing," she replied.

When I took Mom home, I offered to sit with her while she got all the way undressed. She took off her slacks and I saw her swollen ankles, which can be a sign of heart failure.

Something happened in our eyes that damp Sunday evening. We held each other's gaze a few beats longer than usual. Tuesday we would go back to Dr. Shell.

ANOTHER EVENING, LISA was spending time with her family. I sat in Mom's room while she took a shower. Just sat there to make sure nothing happened. I spent my time looking at the photos under the glass on her dresser, and then I lay down on her bed in a fetal position. Mom was facing loss of a different kind again. Loss of getting out of bed and walking down the hall. She could not do it if not for the blessing of Lisa.

HALF MY BRAIN was afraid all the time. I began to put the thoughts into words in conversations with my friends.

"I think I have low-grade mourning," I told Connecticut Marcia, who has known me since I wouldn't share dot-to-dot books with her.

"Do you see a therapist?" asked Sarah, my genius friend and website family-history-business partner.

I was uncomfortable. It felt like my stomach had one foot in the grave. I wrote "breathe" on my calendar.

"My levees broke yesterday," I told Mom.

"I know," she said. "I knew it was coming."

"It's good," I said, getting teary again.

"I know," Mom said, meaning "I'm not so sure that it is."

"There's a phrase for it," I told her. "Anticipatory grief."

"That's a very good phrase," she said while we let ourselves in on our own secret. I felt selfish, crying to her about her, about bringing up the inevitable, something I don't even bring up to myself.

"I worry about you," my mother told me.

"Me, too," I said, chest-heave sobbing. "When the lights go out, I don't know how I'll be."

"You'll be strong by then," she said. "You'll be ready. When I'm ninety-two, you'll be ready."

"Why so soon? Why just ninety-two?"

"Okay, ten years. Ten years from now."

"By then I'll be in an Alzheimer's unit myself," I said. "So I won't even care."

OUR OUTINGS ARE to the Coumadin Clinic, down a long gray hallway past Dr. Shell's office, where my mother gets her blood levels checked. The clinic has a small waiting room, a microcosm of the world we live in now. We are textbook examples of the Designated Daughter species: old mothers, adult daughters, wearing out like flannel.

The getting in and out of the car is an ordeal for

Mom, but we've got it down to a science: I drive her
car; I stop at the double-doored back entrance, low-
energy-operated for the handicapped. Whenever I
saw that sign, I thought it was the handicapped who
were low-energy, until it dawned on me one day that
it referred to the buttons. I walk Mom under the over-
hang, which my mother and father always referred to
as the "porte cochere." Dad said it with an accent.
Mom says it with quotation marks around it. We walk
one inch at a time to the bench in the hallway. I run
back to the car, park it, and run through the double
doors to get my mother and bring her up in the elevator to the second floor. Necessity is the mother of
getting over elevator phobia. Mom sits and I sign her
in. I carry her purse and pay her copay out of her
wallet.

The Coumadin Clinic is our observation deck.
We take a number and watch the world.

There we were in the waiting area when Gordon
Schiffman, a friend of my parents, came in.

"How are you, Gordy," my mother said.

"Good to see you, Phyllis," said Gordon.

Mom held number 26; Gordon was number 27.
Number 25 was taking a long time. Close quarters,
doctor's office, stale flu-ridden air, thick and nox-
ious, like that of an airplane. Another daughter
joined her mother in the waiting room and read the
paper.

"This weather!" said Gordon.

We were in the midst of an unseasonably beautiful spell.

"Oh, this weather!" Mom answered. "If it weren't for this weather," and she put her finger to her head like a pistol. "Days of Grace, Bob used to call days like these." She turned and looked at me. "Remember, Debba? Days of Grace, Daddy used to call them."

These have been my Days of Grace, or should I say my days of Phyllis. It has been seven years since I came home.

ONE DAY WE were in the car, philosophizing again.

"Nobody ever said they wished they spent more time . . ." Mom started the sentence.

". . . in the Coumadin Clinic," I finished. Then one Sunday night we found out that Uncle Junior Soprano took Coumadin, too.

I HAD BEEN feeling too weary of mind and heart to handle what was happening. Salt was building up in Mom's body, causing her legs to swell. Her shortness of breath was so severe that she'd called Dr. Shell's nurse, Cornie, and Cornie had persuaded her to come in.

Lisa was at a three-day gathering, long in the making. So I went and did my best and offered to sleep over, but Mom said no. She kept gaining water weight from a change in medication. I urged her to allow that it sucked.

My head was exploding. Her body was a chemistry set. Something had sapped her energy and amped mine.

"I got pissed yesterday," I said to Vineyard Marcia. "Plain annoyed." I repeated whatever annoyance I had found during that particular day. "Just *annoyed*," I said through gritted teeth.

"Good," she answered.

Anticipatory grief has a cumulative effect, just like the new gloss Cindy was putting into my fraying hair. I was prickly, back in black hair. One color.

"You look like you," Vineyard Marcia told me when she and Connecticut Marcia came to visit and comfort me.

"A mother is different than a father," Vineyard Marcia said. Her dad died, while running, when he was fifty-four. "When I lost my father," she went on, "I lost part of my foundation. When I lost my mom, it was like losing part of my body."

When their mother was dying of cancer five years ago, Marcia's sister, Nancy, was the Designated Daughter. Nancy lived closer. Nancy was more aligned with their mother's sociable style. Marcia is a fascinating photographer but a bit reclusive, like me, and lives on an island. The sisters, their mother,

Rose, and their brother, Mark, stepped naturally into this end-of-life relationship. Marcia was there at the bedside when her mother died. When my friend called to tell me that, the finality floored me. I melt down every time I think about it. I let tears come and become thankful for laundry to do. I claw my way through my clutter and weeds in an attempt to put my house in order.

MOM TOOK ANOTHER large step downward in the ego slide of the older woman. The physical-pain doctor told her one thing she could do was buy a cane. A cane store up at the end of her street had flowered canes that were a little too sad Carnaby Street for me, so we decided to take a field trip to a downtown medical-supply store.

"It'll be an adventure," she said, as I reminded her that we'd definitely get lost. I hopped into the driver's seat, and we went west on Broad Street, looking for an address on Fifth Street when we should have been looking for Fifth Avenue. We ended up at the rusty gates of a manufacturing company on its last legs. I told her we could buy crack there if we wanted.

"How do you know about buying crack?" she said.

I think this is when I initiated talk again about the cute cane hunt that had become our day.

"Does cane shopping make you mad?" I asked her.

"A little," she said.

We turned right, then left at the light, then right at the next one. We found ourselves in the Cadillac showroom for the infirm.

"Cars of the future," I told her as we walked through the there-but-for-the-grace-of-God wheelchairs and scooters and seated shopping carts and chairs that lift you up and push you out. Mom had heard of a restaurant in a hip nearby neighborhood, and we were planning to have lunch after the cane. This medical-supply store had the very same Carnaby Street canes they had up at Mom's corner, so she kept the one she had. We found the restaurant and ate a delicious lunch in the arty pub.

"See, it's not about the cane," I told her.

"To me it is," she said.

FACING REALITY ANOTHER day, we discussed Mom's funeral food. We decided on Suzanne, our favorite caterer. We had been at a relative's celebration of life and had loved the spread, which Suzanne had made. Fruit, egg salad, chicken salad, delicious, and miniature coconut cupcakes. Mom isn't allowed to eat coconut, which has always been her favorite thing. I brought two cupcakes to the chair where she sat, thinking I'd eat both, but she fooled me. She snatched one off my plate. I spent a few minutes in the front doorway with the Designated Daughter as she greeted everyone she knew. It was a beautiful summer day, and the community had come to celebrate a life, eat cupcakes, and drink cocktails.

After I dropped Mom off at her house, I thought about the fresh strawberries and the ripe raspberries, how bright and juicy they were, seasonal fruit. If this were exactly the spread that we wanted—fresh strawberries and raspberries—I would be standing in the doorway, sad in the summertime, too.

MOM WAS TOO tired for her first cane lesson.

"That's what happens," I said as I looked at her, shrinking in her blue cashmere sweater right in front of my eyes. I tried to make Fred Astaire jokes, and we laughed weakly. I felt compelled to say I'd be okay if you-know-what. I meant, "if you want to die," but I couldn't form the words.

I called my brother on my way home to wish him a happy birthday. He had already talked to her, learned the cane lesson had been canceled, and wanted to know what was going on, in country.

My friend Lindsey sent me an e-mail: "How is your mother?"

I answered: "My mom is betterish from her cough, but now dealing with low blood pressure and sodium issues. She weighs 105. What the fuck?!"

"I'M NOT READY to die," Mom told me one day, reading my mind. And I told her, in words this time, that if she wanted to, she could. I'd be okay, and this time I believed it. It was the least I could do for her.

"Oh, you will," she told me. "You will, I know it."

"Let your will be my will," I said, the same prayer I said to God in the morning.

When Nana was dying, she had a dream that all her friends were waiting for her in heaven, and they were wearing housecoats.

"Mother, in heaven they'd be wearing mink coats, not housecoats," my mother told her.

MOM HAD HER first cane lesson on the physical-therapy floor in yet another building on the Mount Carmel medical center campus, which is practically in her backyard. When well-meaning friends and relatives—and I—urged her to move out of that great big house, when factoring this and factoring that, we always put proximity to Mount Carmel and Dr. Shell at the top of the "pros" list. She met me in the hall in a blazer and chinos, singing "Tada tada tada" and moving her cane sideways, vaudevillian-style. "All I need is a bowler," she said.

At physical therapy, she had to walk laps around the room, climb steps, try to balance on one leg, and walk while looking to the right and to the left. She was doing great today. She looked beautiful and as ready for life as the spring bulbs blooming. I sat watching, holding our purses. The therapist told her that her cane—the floral one we went on the wild goose chase for—was too long. He took out his cloth tape measure. I held one end down; he pulled up the other. "She needs twenty-eight inches," he said to me, still kneeling. I was thinking we would have to go to a little people's store online, but we returned to the first cane store. Mom had not taken the price tag off the cane yet, so however good she may have looked at the lesson, her cane looked absent-minded. The cane store was empty except for two friends trying on support hose and the saleswoman, who did have a cane that swiveled down to twenty-eight inches. The handle was a little different, but one of the support-hose ladies said her husband had one and liked it, so we opted for the peppy floral number. There was a price difference of three dollars, but the saleslady waived the difference, we thanked her, and we were off to another lunch. We couldn't do Bob Evans again, so we went down the road to a dark restaurant where patrons were still allowed to smoke. It was the second beautiful spring day in a row, and we found ourselves in a booth in the back room.

"Siberia," I said.

We had chosen to come to a cave and felt the mistake descending as we looked over the menu. The hostess escorted in a heavy man with sleepy eyes; he was with his mother, too. They sat together, not speaking. The waitress came, they ordered, they sat, not speaking. She looked prim, slightly dressed up, as if this were a Sunday instead of a Tuesday. "I just could not stay stuck in the house today, Mike," she said.

Their food came, they ate, and Mike began to listen to his mother. We paid up and walked out to the car, back into the beautiful day.

"Fucking cane," Mom said.

ON A GLOOMY, gloomy Sunday, when all was right in my world, I felt completely capable of managing for myself. D.G. came out in the early afternoon with soup from Panera for me, a bagel and coffee for her. We had a lovely visit. We hadn't seen each other in the flesh since early in the week. We looked good to each other, I think. After she left, I read from Abigail Thomas's *Safekeeping* and was inspired by the writer and the writing. Soon it would be time to get dinner, and then I would not be capable.

Lisa had left me a tuna noodle casserole, soup and sandwich, and fruit and custard; my refrigerator was the Automat, a Horn & Hardart. For me, it seemed just as far away and equally difficult to get to. My legs and back were so painful when I walked, and I was so "tippy," that when I got back to the safety of my sitting room and my tray table, I was huffing and puffing. I felt almost ashamed of being old and weak and wished I had persisted in the physical therapy.

I admit to my age, I say it proudly, but it sure as hell is a pain to be eighty-seven.

Failing is not the choice we ever consciously make. I remember a child, not one of ours, who, in preschool, "failed" in the administration's eyes at the skill of sandbox. (Although I believe one little Greene did get a "does not play well with others.") It seemed so ridiculous at the time, grading babies. None of us wants to fail at anything, but we all do, and if it's done kindly, we might as well learn it early. You don't need to get an A in everything. I confess that I have pretty much failed at cooking and sewing and, to be truthful, many of the domestic skills except the important ones: mothering, enveloping, supporting, encouraging, loving. These, I hope, I did right. But now I know I am physically failing, which is a bitter pill to swallow—along with the nineteen others I take daily. It is beyond my control, and I want to be gracious as others do for me, but it is not what I would have chosen.

Almost one year to the day after the living room bounce, after five intermittent helpers, four visits to the internist, three X rays, two aborted rounds of physical therapy, two "alarmingly low" sodium levels, two bouts of bronchitis, one consultation at the Spine Institute and one orthopod, it was time to call "uncle." When I called, I got Lisa. That is, I got a miracle.

One of my excellent intermittent helpers, Felica, was unavailable when D.G. and I realized we had to have help, immediately, that weekend. Felica recommended Lisa. When she arrived that first weekend, I was miserable and in bed again. As soon as she walked in the door, I felt better, having her in the house. In the course of the weekend, she told me that she had moved back to Columbus recently and was looking for a place to live. By Sunday afternoon I said to her, "I met you in the morning, and I am asking you to marry me by night." Living in the lower level of the house, she helps me a certain number of hours a week: drives to markets and doctor's appointments, fills my weekly medicine boxes, helps me with my clothes, runs errands, is my computer guru and my COO on house repairs. She picked out my new dryer and my petunias and planted them; she makes my meals; she stands by while I shower; and she still has time for her own life, which is communicating in American Sign Language, in the public ministry as one of Jehovah's Witnesses. As she tried to explain what she did for me to an English couple at her congregation, they grasped it in a minute: "Oh," they said, "you are her au pair."

It pains me to remember that, not so long ago, I could do all of those things for myself. So I don't think about it—much.

I am lucky and I am realistic, but being a stay-at-home mom is not my cup of tea; my preference would be a nice vodka martini before dinner, with olives, in a white-tablecloth restaurant.

I truly empathized with a TV panelist, urbane, bright, and successful—and not that old—who completely forgot Saddam Hussein's name in the middle of a comment. It happens to all of us, but it can drive a person buggy to wait for a "lost" name to arrive, unexpectedly, in the brain. One morning before I got up, and only barely awake, I thought of my college roommate and, for no special reason, remembered that she had once told me her husband had said of their son's "hippie" wedding—thirty-some years ago—that it was a good thing that Peggy's father and his sister—his sister, what was her name?—it wouldn't come to me—that it was a good thing they were no longer living to witness the barefoot bride and the groom clad in homespun. All the next day, that nameless sister haunted me. As I was brushing my teeth on the second night, "Deveara" rang out in my head. Of course, of course, Bus's sister was named Deveara. That is not likely to ever be a name I'll need to know again, but still, how I wish I hadn't had to struggle so to find it. Once I remembered Deveara, that little data bank in my head reminded me of what Bus wholeheartedly believed, which has helped us all over a lot of bumps. "They don't give any medals in the middle of the race," Bus always said, meaning "Keep going. It ain't over till it's over." Now, from my vantage point, I can see clearly that it ain't.

With age, to get something done is to think through your moves carefully. Getting up in the morning, I must remember to take my cell phone and glasses from the nightstand to the dresser, so I can pick them up on my way to the sitting room from the bathroom. We are talking a distance of fewer than ten steps. Before my health let me down, I used to make that trek ten times a day. One week I realized that I had not been out of my cave—my bedroom, bathroom, and sitting room—from Tuesday until Friday. Lisa had bought a few fresh yellow Alstroemeria for the living room on Tuesday. What a lovely surprise when I made my way to the front of the house Friday noon.

Even with a functioning mind, you need to review the facts and have all the papers in front of you as you engage a utility company or order from an 800 number. How many times have I walked from desk to purse to address book, phone in hand, trying to find my credit card or the item number or the ID number. Even when you know a child is going to call and there are a few things you want to remember for that conversation, you write it down beside the phone—and then forget to mention it after all!

I feel as if my grade should be C— in sandbox, and too much of the time, I don't even want to play with others.

But Debby keeps giving me A; for effort, I guess.

And that has made all the difference.

10

BONUS YEARS

*A*NONPROFIT ORGANIZATION IN town held a fund-raiser where people wrote tributes to the women they love. Mom decided to write one. I asked her why.

"I wanted to do it for you," she said. "And really, I want to show off the granddaughters."

We'd had an "in-gathering" the summer before on the Fourth of July, and the whole family was together. Tim sent a blow-up pool, since the pool where we had spent a lifetime of summers was no longer there. Mom met Zach. To me, this was like seeing the hands touching on the ceiling of the Sistine Chapel. Mom willed her body to bend. She sat down on the floor of her sitting room and held Zachary in her lap. She had taken out a picture book she'd saved from grandmothering, and read it to our new little boy.

I asked Maggie what I should have on hand to make the trip easier. I didn't want her to have to schlep everything on the plane.

Her e-mail flashed me back to all the responsibility of mothering: "Thank you for offering to alleviate some of the stress in packing for the family trip. It would be wonderful if there were some diapers and wipes and food for him. I will pay you back once we're there—just give me the receipts."

What is she, kidding? I saved the receipt. Plan to scrapbook it someday.

"He wears Huggies size 3. I use Seventh Generation wipes but would be happy with anything (the less scented and more natural the better). He eats Gerber cereals (single-grain). He eats all three types: rice, oatmeal, and barley. One box would be sufficient, though. I mix his cereal with Horizon-brand organic formula. It comes in a red can."

I used to feed her fried hot dogs in butter and felt that *that* was too much work.

"He eats jarred baby food (no, I don't make my own). I typically buy Earth's Best brand or Gerber Tender Harvest (both organic). He can eat stage 1 or 2. He will eat: carrots, peas, sweet potatoes, apples, apricots, pears, peaches, squash. Any mix of these is

fine. I am sure he will have added more to his reper-
toire by then. He eats about 2–3 jars a day."

I bought the gentle baby detergent Dreft, too.
When was the last time you bought Dreft?

We had a professional photographer come to Mom's
backyard, and he took pictures of our family together,
which—the morbid mind continues the sentence—
may be for the last time. We did all the combination
shots you would at a wedding. Timmy's family. Bobby's family. Maggie's family. Mom and me. The photographer took a shot of the three granddaughters:
Maggie, Amanda, and Hannah. These cousins all
look alike and are not hard on the eye.

Mom knew that at the tribute, they'd flash the
Greene granddaughter picture, among others, across
a huge screen.

Mom wrote:

> My tribute is to the hopeful future of the women
> in my family, intuiting that somehow I literally
> see it in their faces. I celebrate my three grand-
> daughters, envisioning Hannah in high school,
> becoming Amanda, at work in publishing in
> New York, becoming Maggie, my pride, mother
> of my first great-grandchild, becoming a strong
> woman like her mother, my daughter, D. G.
> Fulford, who embraces the greater world with
> her TheRememberingSite.org (she promised

she'd work in an ad) while enriching my world, right here, as my rock and support and best friend.

THE TRIBUTE COMMITTEE chose Mom's essay as one of the best in the mother/daughter category. She would read hers from the stage behind a scrim. I was to be spotlighted in the audience.

"You think I should brush my hair?" I asked Mom.

"Just don't wear that pink sweater with the holes in it," she said.

Lisa, Mom, and I got to the crowded venue, and the tribute people led Mom off to her role as a silhouette. They loved the flowery cane, *loved it,* and thought Mom should lean on it jauntily, backlit, which she dutifully did. After her tribute, she came out from behind the scrim so the audience could see her.

The DVD of the tribute came in the mail. Viewing it upset Mom. "I will never, ever appear in public where I have to walk," she said. "I had no idea. I'm an old, old woman. Round-shouldered. I'm the humpbacked grandmother getting off the plane in the Fosamax ad."

"Well, like Jill told me, look at it in a few years, and you'll think you look great," I said.

"No. I'm not kidding. This was upsetting," she

said. She had just seen herself from across a room.

"I suppose if I hadn't seen you in a while, I'd notice," I say. "And we know there's the trouble walking. Was it the cane you hated?"

"Everything," Mom said. "I am so small and stooped over. I look tiny standing next to the director. I saw myself, and I'm an old woman."

"You don't sound old, nothing in your voice comes across as old, and—"

My mother stopped me. "I didn't tell you this to have you say nice things to me," she said. "This was really, truly upsetting to me. I'm going to throw it away. I don't even want you to see it."

THIS IS MIND'S-EYE dysmorphia. We feel younger than we look. The realization comes slowly that maybe, just maybe, we don't have all the time in the world. This is presented to Designated Daughters in different ways almost every day. While others see Mom's radiant, shining self, she sees a stooped-over old woman leaning on a cane. Clarity comes, bringing with it things we don't want to see.

I called Patti to join our high school friend Diny and me for lunch.

Patti said, "Hold on. What, Mother?" She yelled, "No!" and got back on the phone. "She asked me if

I didn't think I needed to get my bangs cut before meeting you two."

DINY'S MOTHER DIED years ago, in her early sixties. It bothered Diny that she never dreamed about her mother, and she longed to. I tried to have her ask the new moon for dreams of her mother, but the moon was letting her down. Then she had a dream that she and I and Vineyard Marcia were walking along and Diny couldn't get us to listen. She shouted to us in the dream; the most adamant commandment, "My mom wants to talk to you."

We turn to our mothers for power, even in death.

WHENEVER VINEYARD MARCIA and Connecticut Marcia come to visit, one of their first stops is to see my mother. They talk about her glow. It's there, though not visible in that stupid DVD. My mom is incandescent. Everybody says so. Safe with my friends, on my screened porch, my tears flow freely again. They are there to allow me to debrief, to decompress. I have been living on high alert, poised every minute of every day for a final phone call or a rush to the hospital. I have stopped listening to music. It makes me too emotional. NPR is all I can handle, and really, really low. I am consumed with catastrophic thoughts. High alert takes a physical, mental, and emotional toll. I am hypervigilant, fighting *and* flighting all my life. I added fish oil and B vitamins to my diet and promised myself I'd exercise, which, for a time, I did.

A NEW BOB Evans sprang up on Mom's corner. We drove there, discussing how good it was not to be calling Quality Pool to come open the pool for the summer. When we pulled into the new Bob Evans parking lot, looking for a handicapped space, we saw a Quality Pool truck parked at the restaurant, too.

I took pancakes, she took crepes.

I went to the bathroom, Mom went to pay at the counter. A very exotic-looking woman was working there. This was going to be nothing like the old Bob Evans! I met Mom, and she was saying, "I don't understand," and the exotic woman tried to explain once again: "The kid is diclinned."

Mom was using some kind of Bob Evans—issued card to pay the check. I think it was a gift certificate from one of her good-humored friends who met her there for lunch.

I said, "Excuse me?" to the exotic woman.

"The kid is diclinned."

"The card is declined," I told my mother.

Mom started customer-servicing with the woman, telling her the kid could not be diclinned.

I just started laughing. Laughing and laughing. Mom did, too, then, laughing and coughing. We felt

better than we had when we came in. We stumbled
out the door, roaring each word like Inspector
Clouseau. "Diclllinned, decliiiined," we said. Home
again, home again, jiggedy-jog.

ALONG WITH ALL the hard parts, there are crocuses
in the snow. Happy events that keep you going. One
day Mom called. She'd just been on the phone with
the president of Franklin University. After her thirty
years on the board, they wanted to award her an hon-
orary doctorate.

Dr. Phyl!

She talked about how meaningful the Franklin
graduations are, saying that many of the graduates
were adults, often the first in their family to attend
college. She talked about the babies in the audience
and the sounds of children cheering their mothers.
And then the university president called her back.
Would she be the Franklin University commence-
ment speaker?

This would be in May. My brothers would come.

"Has anybody ever given it sitting down?" I asked.
"And what if it's hot, and that's a heavy robe."

"If Franklin Delano Roosevelt can do it, I can do
it," my mother said.

I GOT TO California again. Zachary will likely never
remember this trip, but I will never forget it. We

played birds and nest, and I met Dora the Explorer.

"*Vámonos, amigos!*" Zach said as he ran down the hall.

In the morning he called, "Memaw, Memaw, are you awake?" I dashed in to see him—it jolted my body to move fast in the morning—he stood smiling in his crib. Maggie told me that some mornings, he'd yell, "Helllooooooo, helllooooooo, people!"

He asked Mommy who her best friend was. Mommy said Daddy. He asked Daddy who his best friend was. Daddy said Mommy. Zach asked Mommy who Memaw's best friend was. Mag smiled at me, truly knowing her solitary mother. "Memaw is Memaw's best friend," she said.

I had finally reached the pinnacle preached by Mildred Newman and Bernard Berkowitz in their 1971 celebration of self: *How to Be Your Own Best Friend.* After thirty-five years, I'd evolved.

ONE NIGHT DURING my visit, Zach had a bad dream.

"What was it about?" I asked him.

"Elephants," he said.

I DID NOT get sick this trip. I wore a pharmaceutical mask on the plane. I liked the look. It showed off my eyes, my best feature. And it prevented me from having to talk. I began to notice couples, not just mothers and their Designated Daughters, and realized I hadn't had a thought without my mother in it for eight years. On the last leg of the flight, I sat next to a woman wearing two hats, the top one knit to look like the American flag. When we touched down in Columbus, she said to me, "Praise Jesus, He's the only one!" She had flown all the way from London, all the way with Jesus, and He had brought her home. I nodded to her vigorously and gave her a thumbs-up. Praise, praise. I get down on my knees after every trip and kiss my living room floor.

MOM GOT A card from Macy's—an invitation, she said, to come to a special event in the makeup department. Mom is not a makeup woman, but I think she believed this would be a pick-me-up for me because I keep making face-lift faces in the mirror. All the Harmon women had gone off to a spa together, and I could see Mom's mind working. This would be the same thing locally!

So began our outing to meet the fabulous face designer who was the draw for the event. We chatted and drank the bottled water that Macy's gave us until the designer swooped onto the floor. He may have been wearing a cape, but if he wasn't, he sure gave the cape impression. We watched him work and then send the guest, laden with product, over to one of Macy's beauty consultants behind the register in a white doctor's coat. Mom took her turn, then I got up to the designer's stool. I couldn't see Mom because my head was blocked by the designer's head. When I caught up to her (I was untransformed, alas), I saw she was hugging the consultant and they both were crying.

"What were you talking about?" I asked, charging my new black eyebrow mascara—think Groucho Marx—on my Macy's card.

"Mothers and daughters," she said. We held hands, walking out. She looked at me. "You look good," she said, "but I look like a hundred-year-old hooker."

EIGHT YEARS AFTER Dad died, Mom decided she wanted TO THINE OWN SELF BE TRUE engraved on the headstone under our family name. When she first told me about her plan, I was a little surprised. First of all, I hadn't even known she was thinking of a memorial quotation, and after all this time together, I thought I knew everything in her head. I tried to argue with her selection. I thought "To Thine" was a little ordinary. I would have thought she'd have gone with Latin. Or maybe "Do justice, love mercy, and walk humbly with Thy God." She'd always liked that. I tried to grab the engraving as an assignment. I'd come up with something esoteric, something Delphic, even, to sell the steak and sizzle of our ancestry. I thought perhaps Bob Dylan's "Do what you can do and do it well" but, on further consideration, found it too admonishing.

I BROUGHT THE picture of my beautiful grandson to the cemetery the day Mom told me about the engraving. I had weatherproofed it in a Baggie to leave at the headstone for Dad. I held Mom's forearm tightly as we inched our way down the slope to the car after our time graveside. Eight years we'd been coming. Thirty-two seasons. We'd placed flags and stones and pennies and chrysanthemums and one horrifying floral grave blanket there with Dad. We'd take small day trips to our final destination, and then we'd go out to brunch.

It has been eight years of change, of acceptance, of support and understanding. I arrived back in Columbus not knowing what "need" meant and what I specifically could offer. Now I knew my steady grip under my mother's forearm was enough.

She was right, of course. "To thine own self be true" is perfect. Nobody is going to judge you here. Be who you are. What more self-assuring message could be sent to our descendants? What more satisfying reminder to be read by me?

I DON'T HAVE a cemetery plot. I just plan to jump in beside Mom and Dad.

"Probably the day of your funeral," I told Mom.

"Oh, I just wish they'd sprinkle me on top of Daddy," she said. "It's not like there are going to be separate beds."

THE PAST EIGHT years I have known—and how often in your life do you know this?—that I have been at the right place at the right time doing the right thing. I was needed. I delivered. And I received.

I have learned to know what I have while I have it. That time can be both finite and infinite. Mom and I know independence intimately, and we know interdependence, too: the growth and growing pains that last a lifetime between a mother and a daughter. I came doubting I could handle any of it. I now know I can handle it all.

"I FEEL GOOD," she said this morning.

My heart leaped. "You feel good?"

"I feel good," she said.

"Is this . . ." and I said her phone number.

(I find myself punching this phone number into my microwave. I use her key to try to open my front door.)

She repeated my small joke to Lisa, and they both laughed.

"I'm multitasking," my mother told me. "I'm putting on my lipstick."

"Why?" I asked.

"The nurse!" she told me. I had forgotten. A nurse was coming to see if her long-term health insurance, which she expensively and wisely signed up for, would now kick in. Now that she really could not make it down that hall and into that kitchen and back to that chair.

"Take off your lipstick!" I told her. "You want to look bad. You want that drawn, deathy look. Don't dress up and be your fabulous self. Take off your bra and look feeble."

"Oh, Debby," she said, meaning "Don't be ridiculous."

"I'm not kidding," I told her.

"But what can I do about my glow?" my mother asked.

"Think impacted bowels," I told her.

She told me she was going to wipe off her lipstick.

She felt good. My prayers were answered once again.

WHEN MY FAMILY moved to California all those years ago, we were introduced to the concept of a bonus room, a room that could be used for anything, a room not restricted by description. Not a bedroom. Not a den. A bonus room! This was so exciting, like a Cracker Jack prize in your house. Forget about the kitchen! Forget about the yard! Forget square foot-age! Show us the bonus room, whatever it was; it sounded like fun and hope and promise.

These years have been a bonus room. Bonus years I never expected or thought about: in some ways, the most important in my life.

When I was in first grade, in Mrs. Sutton's class, I wrote a Mother's Day poem that was put to music by Mrs. Hilyard, the music teacher. I do not know how I got the words out. My mother was in the audience. I stood in front of the classroom, blue dress, dark socks, and knobby knees, my neck folded paralyzed, attached to my left shoulder. I was a duck hiding its beak in winter, but I sang.

Mothers are sweet and mothers are kind.
When you are bad, they really don't mind.
They buy you things, they love you so
They take you where you want to go.

I think at the time I was waxing lyricial about my mother buying me things at the drugstore and tak-ing me where I wanted to go, like the drugstore for another thing. But I was prescient, instinctive, and eternal (if I do say so myself). My song came from a voice so deep inside me that I didn't know it was there. The me of me. The part that knows.

Transformation happens somewhere between instinct and osmosis. If you walk beside your mother when she needs you, you'll absorb her wisdom and her strength. As always, she'll return the favor. Her strength and wisdom will take you as far as you ever want to go.

THE ELEPHANT IS somewhere miles ahead. He got tired of our draggy pace. We got tired of him, hanging around.

So I sat down to write and began: "I shall always be grateful for these bonus years," when it suddenly hit me that I shan't always be—anything. I imagine myself living on and on, laughing with D.G., going to the Coumadin Clinic, stopping to say hello to Cornie, Dr. Shell's nurse, and Sharon, his receptionist, our friends. Then going to Bob Evans, where Debby will eat pancakes and I will order the crepes filled with cream cheese and fruit. In my mind, we will do this forever. But somewhere ahead, there is an end.

What if we did not have these years in which to delight? Not everyone does. In some strange way, I am practicing to go, and I think Debby is practicing to live without me. They say there is no dress rehearsal for life; for death, maybe. It is the neat trick Debby and I are trying to pull off. This time is a gift to the mother and the daughter; this *is* the rehearsal. There. I have said it, and I am not afraid.

Well, perhaps a little. When I went for a regular checkup of my seven-year-old pacemaker, I was not expecting to hear that the battery needed changing. Soon. I was given all the appropriate instructions: what blood tests I would need, when to stop eating (midnight the night before), and all the other routine orders. When I looked more closely at the preadmission physician order form, one blank that had been filled in by the scheduling nurse read "diagnosis: end of life." I confess that it gave me a start until I realized it was describing the equipment and not the patient.

During those six endless days after Gerald Ford's death, I watched Betty Ford while they buried her husband. From Palm Springs to the Capitol. From the long vigil and the long ceremony to Michigan and the final goodbye, she did everything that was expected of her. Susan, Designated Daughter, was holding her mother's purse when the president walked Betty Ford down the long aisle of the Washington National Cathedral. Betty walked—no cane, no walker, no wheelchair. These we saw only briefly at other times, but as she held the arm of a seemingly uninvolved George W. Bush and looked straight ahead, you could see it in the set of her shoulders: I am a first lady; I remain a first lady.

Looking at her, small and shriveled, you wondered how that emaciated, frail body—how all of us, with our little shrinking outsides—could contain such tenacity, integrity, ability. Betty showed the whole world that we can. It was an inspiration to watch.

To hell with Shakespeare's seven ages of man. We may be sans teeth or sans eyes, but we are not sans everything; we are still on the road of life, and we outstrip the elephant every day. We will call him when we need him.

For Christmas, Debby brought me a beautiful set of small bronze-ish elephants for the coffee table. I have a crystal ball that is meant to hang on a door and be a sun catcher, but the string pulled out of it long ago. Now I sit these happy elephants in a circle around it. The elephants are playful, and their ears are down, which I read as a good sign.

EPILOGUE

WE'D JUST COME from *The Devil Wears Prada*, which we loved, and were sitting in the car in my driveway, talking, before I dropped Mom at her friend's house for Nathan's hot dogs and potato salad. It was Independence Day weekend, and no one was coming home. We talked about the next time we might have an in-gathering. Evvybuddy, as my Zach would say.

For my ninetieth, Mom said.

Or my sixtieth, I suggested.

"When I'm ninety you'll be sixty, it's the same year," Mom said.

We laughed laughs of astonishment, incredulation, and celebration.

And it was only three years away! Oh my God, three years.

We sat in my car in the driveway on the Fourth of
July, laughing at the wonder of it all. It was a moment you couldn't catch in a camera. And it's the way
I want to remember my mother and me for the rest
of my life.

ACKNOWLEDGMENTS

WE ARE FOREVER grateful to Rebecca Gradinger at Janklow & Nesbit Associates, who immediately saw the significance, and to Ellen Archer, Pamela Dorman, Kathleen Carr, and E. Beth Thomas at Voice, who took our words and gave them wings.

A B O U T   T H E   A U T H O R S

D. G. Fulford is the bestselling author of several books, including the classic *To Our Children's Children: Preserving Family Histories for Generations to Come*, which she wrote with her brother, Bob Greene. She is also the cofounder of therememberingsite.org, which helps people tell their life stories. D.G.'s mother, Phyllis Greene, became a first-time author at the age of eighty-two with *It Must Have Been Moonglow: Reflections on the First Years of Widowhood*, a bestseller. She is the mother of three, the grandmother of eight, and the great-grandmother of two. Fulford and Greene live in Columbus, Ohio.

Readers may contact D. G. Fulford at dgfulfordbooks@aol.com and Phyllis Greene at phgbooks@aol.com.